# LEADING
## THE WAY UP
## MT. OLYMPUS

How Acts of Leadership Help People Become Successful

## DR. STEVE BROE

March 2015

To my Favorite Mad Scientist, Jack, thanks for your Friendship, Steve

ISBN: 1511439181
ISBN 13: 9781511439183
Library of Congress Control Number: 2015905355
CreateSpace Independent Publishing Platform
North Charleston, South Carolina

# Acknowledgements

I am grateful for my friends and colleagues who have always believed in my work and my passion. I believe that leaders make the world a more exciting, valuable place. These people helped me keep going.

To my friends in the *National Speakers Association, Arizona Chapter,* you gave me your time, ideas and a sense of community. You told me that it was possible to change my life and my work, to do that work I am passionate about.

To my friends Dan Robertson, Will Jones and Daniel Valenzuela you met with me nearly every week for the last two years and gave me emotional support and strategies to create my work faster and with meaning. Thank you.

To my editor, Jake Poinier of More Cowbell Books, you helped make this work shine! Thanks for your time. You brought joy and expertise to the challenge of getting the words right.

I have many friends in District 3 Toastmasters who have influenced my growth and career change. They have continued to say "YES" to everyone who imagines using more of their talent professionally. Some but not all of these special people include David Hodesh, Nancy Goins, Terry Lee, Steve Gottry, Bettie Covington, Holly King, Connie Kadansky, Don Clausing, Jodie Kay and Stefan Petra.

To my sweetheart and lovely wife Carolyn, I still owe you a trip to London and the land of King Arthur.

# Table of Contents

# Introduction

It is a long way from the bottom to the top.

Traveling up a mountain is vigorous work. Before you hike, you will select your shoes and clothes for the journey. You will need to provision food and water. You probably will not be walking alone, so you will need to make decisions with your companions. If you are camping on your journey to the summit, your need for planning and physical preparation is even more complicated.

When you get to the top of the mountain, you feel satisfied. You know that you have accomplished something. If the experience is sufficiently profound, you'll be a changed person. Working hard, climbing mountains, and reaching goals can do that to you. A changed life follows a vigorous-enough, substantial-enough effort. Even though it is a long way to the top, people willingly hike mountains in order to earn a transformed life.

Within the context of this book, Mt. Olympus represents a significant life effort, specifically in terms of leadership and achieving success. Some people climb Mt. Olympus regularly; they continue to challenge themselves and the people around them to achieve something more. Along the way to the summit, these mountain climbers typically expand all they are capable of doing. They develop a reputation. They may even become legendary.

In Greek mythology, the summit of Mt. Olympus is where the Greek gods (the Twelve Olympians) took up residence. Of course, Mt. Olympus also exists in the real world, the second-highest mountain in the Balkans, in the Olympic range between Thessaly and Macedonia. It has the honor of being the first national park of Greece, as well as being a World Biosphere Reserve.

The first verified ascent of Mt. Olympus occurred in 1913, with the tallest peak known as the Throne of Zeus.

If you are an astronomy buff, you probably know that an enormous shield volcano on Mars is called Olympus Mons. This peak has a very gentle slope, but it is three times as high as Mt. Everest. Olympus Mons would rise nearly 14 miles above sea level (if Mars had a sea); to date, no one has ever climbed it!

Throughout this book, I have adopted the idea of Mt. Olympus as an important life challenge. Someone who has climbed Mt. Olympus has the right to feel successful!

The experience of climbing Mt. Olympus is analogous to the journey it takes to become a leader. In my research, I have talked to many leaders over the last few years; some have climbed their personal Olympian peak and others have summited several. This book is designed to help you use your leadership skills to become successful at what you do.

What does Mt. Olympus mean to you? I have talked to many people who have a big project, a life-changing event, or a business they want to launch. When I listen to people tell me about the challenges ahead of them, I think, "My friend is preparing to climb Mt. Olympus." Yesterday, a business owner told me that she has survived cancer, and now she wants to write a book about her journey. The idea of writing a book is intimidating to her. She has gone through a lot already, but she has selected her next journey to success. Mt. Olympus represents a major life undertaking that will make one feel successful. Do you see Mt. Olympus in your future?

**My Mt. Olympus Climbing Team**

In a very real way, undertaking this book was a Mt. Olympus for me, and I was fortunate to have a diverse team of 35 successful people in creating the study that enabled it. While I didn't ask my respondents their ages, my youngest interview subject was around 20 years old at the time, and had been a cover girl on *Seventeen* magazine. She became successful by launching an internet-based social media business. Later, she sold that business to a larger company. My oldest respondent was over 80. Jack told me that he had started more than 20 businesses in his career, had earned his law degree, and now is focusing on writing books and speaking professionally. He had known and lost wealth—more than once.

The thirty-five respondents for *Leading the Way Up Mt. Olympus* worked in a variety of professions. (You can read the complete details in Appendix I.) The respondents included business leaders, non-profit leaders, owners of businesses, highly placed executives in companies, solo practitioners, speakers, writers, and a physician.

One of the respondents is a past president of Toastmasters International, the not-for-profit famous for building public speaking skills and leadership skills. This respondent now works in his own business, partly as a speaker, writer, and consultant to other professionals.

Another respondent has earned international acclaim as a best-selling author within the self-improvement community. In addition to her writing, she is active in a number of public causes, including working to influence the course of legislation on issues relating to personal responsibility.

Several of the other respondents are writers. One man has written a number of business books. Another writes about prosperity consciousness in addition to being a professional speaker and a religious leader. One gentleman is a sales professional as well as being an author.

I spoke to a number of CEOs of businesses that range in size from less than 10 to several hundred employees across multiple states. Many of these enterprises involve applications of information technology and software. One of the respondents started an advertising business with her son.

I interviewed a number of people who are professional speakers. One is a licensed health care professional who helps dentists use technology for their practices. Several respondents speak on issues relating to human performance. One professional speaker has built her reputation on helping businesses market at conventions.

I talked with a venture capitalist and a philanthropist. I included a banker who specializes in wealth management. One man listed in this study has opened and operates four restaurants.

The physician in this study is a radiation oncologist. He talked to me about the challenge of building a business with other physicians as partners: "No one taught me management skills in medical school." He has pioneered the use of a treatment for tumors (including cancer) that provides an alternative to traditional methods of chemotherapy and surgery, using new technologies. My mind was lifted speaking to this healer about his work!

I believe these 35 successful people have been to the summit of their Mt. Olympus, and they accomplished something big by leading the way to the top. Their story is instructive to anyone who is now facing a mountain, and is preparing to embark. I found that I was in a privileged position by asking them questions about their leadership experience and their journey.

Do you have a big mountain ahead of you? You may feel that you are all alone, that you are going to be taking significant risks, and the trail ahead has its dangers. You may not want to be a leader; you have other reasons for taking this trail. I understand that many reluctant people become leaders because of the challenges they have chosen.

I hope that once you have identified your Mt. Olympus, this book will be your coaching guide to reaching a successful place. Have you been thinking about what will make you successful? I have found that clarity about my destination is helpful, and I am often distracted. I wanted to experience a book about leadership and success for myself. I have found that it is important to develop a crystallized idea of what I am trying to achieve in order to stay on target.

In my view, success generally exhibits four qualities:

1. **Success includes happiness**. Do you dare call your breakthrough a success? I call it hollow and incomplete if the achievement does not deliver happiness.
2. **Success is about financial achievement**. For most of us, success will include a comfortable financial goal.
3. **Success is sustained.** The success state goes on for an extended period and does not have a time limit. For many people, new goals may be set after success is reached, suggesting that the goal setter can achieve new levels of success.
4. **Success is shared**. I think that a successful person must share success in order to be fulfilled. I'm going to include my wife and kids in the experience if I possibly can. Sharing a good thing is important for its value to be worthwhile.

It's also important to recognize what success means to each of us who achieve it. No one believes that a success is simply delivered to a person, like winning a lottery ticket. Common sense and experience show us that a success must be earned by preparatory work.

I believe leadership behaviors and values can push a personal success to a higher level. Leaders change the world of people around them. Many nights I have sat up thinking about what I want to achieve and where I am going. I know that I have 35 new successful friends whom I can reflect on, and consider how they have made important choices for themselves. I find myself asking, "What would my successful friends do if they were here?" The ability to ask that question, and to imagine the guidance from my interview subjects, has been invaluable to me.

I want you to have the benefit of this success guidance too. Successful people do not reach their goals alone. They have had help. The voice of a guide and mentor can help you too.

I am excited that you have bought this book. I want to introduce you to the people who have had an impact on me. I believe their experience of success and leadership is worth the time you are about to invest reading their stories and ideas.

Dream big. You will be able to check your ideas with great leaders who have climbed their mountain already. Your dream of success has powerful motivational energy behind it.

Here's where we are going in this book. We'll start by examining the concept of "success" from the consideration of three different factors: freedom, money, and the mind of a leader. Do you want more freedom? I think that most of us believe that freedom gives us the feeling of happiness. Money is a complicated factor, as money often arrives with responsibilities, which can pull us away from happiness. Success often is related to financial success. We'll talk more about that.

I also discuss the leader's mindset. Success often involves changing the lives of people around you. The skills and talents of leadership can bring greater success for the leader—and for others. Think like a leader, and think about how others can travel with you to success.

Next, we will discuss the essential qualities of leadership. I ask you to think about four qualities:

- Integrity
- Emotional intelligence
- Flexibility
- Courage

We'll spend more time on these four qualities, especially emotional intelligence. A leader usually has a high degree of emotional intelligence, understanding one's emotional composition, as well as the emotional experience of others. Leaders seem to understand the emotional world of the people around them. Some people tell us that emotional intelligence is more closely related to success than is IQ (intelligence quotient). Great leaders are often smart *and* emotionally intelligent.

We will also examine the idea of success and what others have written about it. What is the relationship between happiness and success? Can you have success without financial strength? You will learn about some of the important ideas about what success is, and what some famous people concluded about the topic. Perhaps these ideas of success will help you achieve yours!

Much of this book will examine the ideas of the people I have interviewed. I have taken care to talk to people who represent different walks of life, people who have achieved something exciting and substantive. I have been a good listener to their journey through leadership to success, and I have synthesized related ideas so that you can focus on the big ideas that stand out.

Part of success is simply getting started, and you will have big ideas and guiding principles to think about. The quality of your mind will help you persevere. The ideas that are important to you, in turn, can influence other people to follow you and support your cause. That's what happens when you have led them up a mountain. Leaders imbue the people near them with a sense of vitality and a need for action.

I encourage you to think like a leader, working with integrity and bringing high value to your world. Get excited and take action. Having seen and heard their stories, this is how leaders become successful.

# Chapter 1: Success and Leadership: A Rhapsody

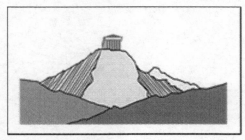

*You have the talent within you to be a leader and to become successful. Your version of leadership and success is unique to you, based on what you have already learned and your innate strengths and emotional character. Learn about what is inside of you so that you can make an impact on the world around you as you climb Mt. Olympus.*

*Mount Olympus was first scaled in 1913 by a solo climber. Successful people do not reach their goals alone. Working as a leader allows you to share your climb with others. Your success helps others to create a better life too.*

Does leadership help someone become successful? My experience in the business world leads me to conclude that the answer is "yes."

It doesn't take a lot of brainpower to see the reason: Leadership is a useful quality, related to career interpersonal influence—and as such, increases the odds of success. Anyone who achieves more with their career, or who expands their influence, is more likely to be successful than someone who isn't. We can predict that skill at math, knowledge of the Vietnamese language, or talent in veterinary science all could improve the odds that someone would be successful in a given field, compared with someone who doesn't have those skills.

Push back a bit further, though. Is leadership *essential* to success? Is a person with such qualities going to be dramatically more successful than someone who isn't? I believe it makes sense to answer "yes" again.

Leadership skill is related to many of the traits that we expect of successful people. The Strengthsfinder model (Rath & Conchie, 2008) describes leadership as a composite of four qualities: execution talent (the willingness to get things done), building a network, influencing others, and thinking strategically. A person who is strong in some or all of these qualities does many of the things we expect in successful people.

Bear in mind, not everyone agrees on what leadership is, let alone the definition of successful.

Financial success is a celebrated, highly visible form. People who have all the money they need may be called successful—and yet I believe you need to go deeper than that. (After all, winning the lottery doesn't indicate anything more than luck.) Will it be there 36 months or 10 years later? A financially successful person has to have learned something important, durable, and repeatable.

An artist may be widely appreciated for his or her music, images, or ideas. The artist has envisioned and created something unique, and shared it with many others. While financial success may or may not follow, the successful artist creates a legacy that other will remember.

The sports star receives publicity, a big paycheck, and social acclaim wherever he or she goes. Sports success may enable a player to leverage a public reputation for business, movies, or television, or a new career as a motivational speaker.

Those are just a few examples, of course. In many cases, high achievement appears to bestow a public glamor or charisma. We take notice when a successful person enters a room, often even when we don't know who they are.

What does success mean for the inner life? Many spiritual teachers claim that the most important change begins within. Imagine a person completely at peace with their life situation and conditions, discovering a passion that drove him or her to do good work in the world. Does this person have a claim on being successful if external life circumstances don't match that inner harmony?

Inner harmony and composure alone aren't enough to be successful, although they may provide a foundation. Success means living a life of abundance, prosperity, and positive social connections – at least in some measure of each.

Conversely, I would argue that an unhappy person is not successful—no matter how profitable the rest of his or her life is. To have all the other trappings of success and *not* be happy, one would seem to have profoundly missed the point. The condition of the soul is important to success.

When you climb your Mount Olympus, you will change your life forever. The achievement of a significant event, such as climbing a legendary mountain, leaves the climber with the forever strengthened with new perspectives on the possibilities of life. Bring others with you on your climb – be a leader.

## FREEDOM TO LIVE LIFE ON PERSONAL TERMS

One useful way to think about success is that a person has the freedom to live a life that he or she defines. Each person's success will be different, depending on what is important to the individual—making the choices and living intentionally as desired. Success in this view is not about money; it is about freedom.

The fact remains, however, that financial means may enable one to live a successful life. My colleague Ted aspires to take the summer off to live anywhere in the world: this year in Spain, exploring the country from an established residence. Success here isn't technically about the money, although he needs enough of it to travel to another continent and set up a temporary home—without a boss, job, or contract restricting how he spends his time or money. He doesn't need to be rich enough to buy an island or a yacht, just wealthy enough to make many personal choices. In fact, he enjoys work enough that his choice of success includes a lifestyle dedicated to working, albeit with the freedom to take the summer off.

There's significant appeal to this version of success: i.e., control over one's own time, personal and business associations, and environment. Not having complete control doesn't mean you're unsuccessful—but could indicate higher potential with greater control over life's limitations. On the one hand, being free to make choices is critical to satisfaction and self-realization. On the other, having freedom and success does not mean a life free of challenges, dry spells, or even reversals of fortune.

## MONEY BUYS YOUR FREEDOM

The Beatles sang about money more than once, such as when they crooned, "Money can't buy me love." Yes, philosophers Paul, John, George, and Ringo knew that money is a poor substitute for the good things in life. Nevertheless, life is easier with the green stuff than without it.

Ask yourself: If money were no object, what would make you feel successful? You probably know that having a lot of money does not make you happy in and of itself. If you suddenly acquired wealth, you would want to buy a few things. After buying a fancy car, beautiful home, and a seaworthy yacht, what you'd probably want most is time.

Free time is an indicator of one's freedom, and money can help you take control of time. Ted doesn't need a lot of money beyond airfare to Madrid. The cost of rent, utilities, insurance, food, and clothing will be approximately the same, whether he lives in Spain or the United States. In fact, for some categories of expenses, his costs may even go down.

The successful person seeks freedom to live a life a unique, personal life. Having lots of money enables some of this freedom. However, money won't make a person unique and vibrant by itself. The difference between a wealthy person and a successful person will be the ability to choose and pursue what he or she wants. Just having money isn't enough; the successful person must create the life of dreams, and this step includes disconnecting from bad choices. The successful person will eliminate some things from his or her life that aren't part of the chosen way to freedom. Old habits and responsibilities may bind a person. The successful person will cast aside parts of life that do not support freedom.

Money may be a starting point for freedom, but you also need to know what you want in order to be free. A schedule won't write itself; certain sacrifices must be made to free up time for the trip to southern Europe.

That's why a specific mental state is necessary for freedom and the experience of success. A person must be willing to make choices and execute on them. Everything cannot happen at once. The right mental state for freedom is willing to say, "I choose this; that will have to come later—or not at all." Money helps to make the best decision possible. When the mind is ready, it is possible to buy freedom.

## HOW IS THE LEADER'S MIND READY FOR SUCCESS?

Now that we've daydreamed a bit about international travel and living the good life, let's turn back to how these factors apply to leadership. A leader is skilled at making decisions, even the difficult or risky ones, or those that may limit future choices. If the leader holds a vision of a positive future, their choices will help to create that success—and failing to choose is not an option.

Leaders have a number of advantages that can help them become successful.

**Leaders continually expand their networks**. Leaders prioritize connecting with new people and building relationships. Exceptional leaders care about the quality of the networks around them, and invest the time and energy to make that a part of achieving their goals.

**Leaders influence the people around them**. Effective leaders shape the opinions and passions of others. That often comes in a vision of a positive future, which can direct the attention of others, gain their commitment, and influence their behaviors. With other people's support, the success of a leader is greatly improved.

**Leaders think strategically**. By planning ahead and considering the obstacles, a skilled leader can allocate resources and improve their advantages. At the same time, a leader will calmly and objectively look for weaknesses in a project, working immediately to change the odds in their favor as well as being flexible in adapting to any new forces that arise.

**Leaders get things done**. The best leaders find ways to create action—focusing on the goal and taking small, medium, and large steps toward it. While others may say, "We need to study this situation further," the leader may ask, "Why wait? We can have the advantage of moving early."

By harnessing the power of people, planning, and execution, leaders have a decided edge in getting results. When applied consistently over time, leaders have an aptitude for being successful. Their minds and actions simply prepare the leader for success.

## DR. STEVE'S TIP

Are you creating the good life, a life of success? Consider your leadership skills as an accelerator to help you achieve your success! Live as a leader, make an impact on your world, and bring other people along with you. Your victory will be all the sweeter.

## REFERENCE

Rath, T. & Conchie, (2008). *Strengths Based Leadership: Great Leaders, Teams, and why People Follow.* Washington DC: Gallup Press.

# Chapter 2: Essential Leadership Skills for Success

*Leaders make an impact around them. You cannot identify a leader by appearance, religion, sexual orientation, or background. You need to look at what they have decided to do, and notice how much things have changed by their actions. Leaders leave a mark. Great leaders build new leaders around them.*

*If you want to be successful, developing yourself as a leader will help you get want you want.*

Because leaders influence other people, we expect them to have a certain number of interpersonal skills and an ability to engage others. Many people have these skills, yet a leader seems to have a combination of skills, character qualities, and other personal characteristics that make him or her effective in most situations. This chapter will examine observable leadership skills and character qualities often associated with leaders.

We also know that leaders, even successful ones, do not have the same combination of skills as other successful leaders. A successful leader is often charmingly unique—no one possesses the exact mix of talents as another. Nevertheless, the list that follows represents an essential recipe of leadership talent.

In addition, there are some internal qualities that are a matter of character. While these qualities (such as integrity) can be developed, matured, practiced, and coached, they cannot easily be studied as established curricula such as accounting or finance. A person's character may be examined, assessed, and challenged, and this may encourage non-leaders to grow and improve their readiness for success through focused attention and discipline.

## LEADERSHIP SKILLS

If you are working on your place as a leader, consider focusing on the following skill areas, which will serve you well in many different conditions. Consider, as well, consulting with a trusted colleague. Adopt a plan to work on one skill at a time, and settle on a list of your top three skill areas for development.

## COMMUNICATION AND PUBLIC SPEAKING

Leaders read and write with impact. In addition, they listen to others around them—which may be even more important than the power of the spoken word, by sending a sincere message to others that "I value you."

Communication is more than sending an outbound message to others; it's about engaging in a dialog. A good leader will be receptive to change based on hearing followers and stakeholders speak.

Public speaking is a special skill that seems to mark the leader, in contrast to those who are reluctant to speak in public. In my work with Toastmasters, I have found that many people never intend to become a leader—but interestingly enough, the transition from "good speaker" to "leader" often seems to emerge as a natural next step without any effort.

## CHANGE SKILLS

Almost by definition, leaders are changing the world around them. (Think about it this way: If the status quo were satisfactory, we would have no need of leaders!) Good leaders recognize that they are bringers of change; somehow, they must bring others with them safely.

Organizations need to change, people need to change, and the leader may need to change, too. This, again, requires a facility in the dynamics of working with people. The change process includes understanding the destination and the powers of influence, as well as the ability to deliver a calming message to others. Change is often disruptive; a good leader shows others that the change will be worth the trouble.

## INNOVATION SKILLS

A changed organization may have a new purpose as well as new ways of working. Innovation alters the way that people interact with the world, and a leader helps others face the small and large adjustments involved. In addition, the leader will support the risk taking that precedes new ways to work. A leader helps to convince others that it is worth the risk to do things in a new way.

An innovative mind-set may include the use of new technologies—and those new tools may cause an uncomfortable shift in how employees view their worlds, or even result in resistance. Leaders help people find the benefits in using innovative approaches to a work process.

## TEAM SKILLS

Even the most talented leaders cannot achieve results by themselves. They build supportive teams around them. Ideally, a labor force extends the intellectual and emotional reach of the leader, because the members usually have internalized the leader's working philosophy—and because they are in practice to become leaders themselves.

Leaders make teams stronger. They encourage teams to become self-sufficient with their leadership skills, and to gain the knowledge and practical experience that adds value to the organization through times of rapid change. A team is a unit force of action, made strong by internal leadership and knowledge.

## TRAINING SKILLS

Leaders change lives, helping people become more effective in the work that they do and sharing and expanding their skills. This includes proficiency in new ways of working. By training people to become more successful in their work, they also become ready for new kinds of assignments or promotions. The leader is rarely the only trainer in most organizations—although leaders are often good at doing this type of work. It's a virtuous circle: Leaders build enterprises in which training is paramount, and people continue to grow.

Training goes beyond specific job skills. It's about educating people to think in new ways, so that their perspectives on work and service continue to expand—transforming them in the process, and even helping them find more depth and meaning in life. Ultimately, proper education and training change what is important to us when we work.

## CHARACTER QUALITIES

A memorable leader is a person of character. Humble leaders won't talk about their character, however the quality of character is revealed daily by choices and actions. Here are some of the character qualities I have found common in leaders.

## INTEGRITY

Leaders may hold different values. (Indeed, we may not even like or agree with their values, but we know that the values define them.) For a person of integrity, however, values are more than just convenient qualities used to make themselves sound good in talking points: The leader consistently acts in accord with the principles of his life, which guide him or her in small decisions and large.

For leaders with integrity, it may be completely irrelevant if anyone else understands that the values are important to them. What *is* important to a leader is a close connection between personal values and the many choices of life, and the behaviors that follow.

## EMOTIONAL INTELLIGENCE

Emotionally stable leaders create a comfortable ambiance through their attitudes and behaviors. By downplaying or eliminating drama, and offering a secure place to talk about the emotional side of life, others can feel secure, even when discussing sensitive material.

Sensitivity to others is one of the gifts of emotional intelligence. The leader with high emotional intelligence is apt to sense the boundaries of comfortable expression and where others' pain points are. Combining sensitivity and shared experiences gives the leader a powerful connection to the attitudes and needs of followers.

Emotionally intelligent leaders are usually aware of their inner emotional experiences and cycles, living authentically, never denying when pain limits their effectiveness. Rather than faking emotional strength, which is easily detected, great leaders don't deny when they are having a rough time—although they may not let a challenge dictate how they will behave. Emotionally intelligent leaders usually live congruently with their inner experiences.

## FLEXIBILITY

I know a wise man and successful executive who describes himself as "rigidly flexible." In other words, he knows what is important for the way he works, he's committed to where he is going, and yet he is always flexible in dealing with other people. I know he won't compromise on matters of principle; he adapts his method of working to the needs of the others around him. It's a savvy way of doing business.

Great leaders offer flexibility to the people around them. They realize that keeping effective people working in their circles is more important than living and working by silly rules.

A flexible leader shows others that *people* and their personal needs are what are important. Of course, a leader has to observe rules designed to protect individuals and the system from chaos. Nevertheless, a leader may find ways to bend the rules, find exceptions, and interpret a situation positively for the people that matter. Flexible thinking, combined with flexible choices and behaviors, allows an observant leader to do remarkable things for the people around him.

In your own experience, you may have witnessed a leader who stood up for a follower, going against tradition or the system; the result was likely a follower who was forever dedicated to that leader. People working for such a leader are highly loyal to the champion who supported them.

## COURAGE

Great leaders are more than flexible; they are also courageous. They take risks in favor of their people or their cause. C.S. Lewis said that courage is not simply one of the virtues, but the presence of every virtue at its testing point. A leader with courage is an unforgettable, unstoppable force.

In the movies, a hero will save someone's life while putting his or her own in peril. Indiana Jones saves the beautiful lady, even though he has to walk through a snake pit. A Marine fights to save a village of farmers. John Wayne challenges the black-hat gang alone on the prairie.

In the workplace, courage may not have any cinematic quality. No one may be there to cheer when the leader stands up to a bad boss or the corporate raider. The courage may go without celebration or any notice at all. People may not know what act of courage has saved them.

Courageous leaders do not need to prove themselves daily—a few interventions may be enough to cement the leader's reputation, and most will not forget the acts when they become known.

Inner courage often means the willingness to think dangerous or bold thoughts, to challenge the wicked, to act strategically when the odds seem dim, or to support a virtuous act while others take a so-called pragmatic view in opposition. The leader with inner courage is willing to do the right thing—even when it appears unreasonable to do so.

It's especially telling when executives make decisions that hurt them personally—for example, when a manager makes a commitment that pays off in five years, instead of five weeks. The hallmark of inner courage is a solid sense of value coupled with a very long view: the willingness to forgo short-term gains in exchange for a better future.

Inner courage may not always make sense, but it is attractive to people. Values are important, and when people find themselves subjected to decisions based on compromise, they admire someone who takes a solid stand. Making a firm decision does not mean that leaders sacrifice themselves over their positions. Leaders are practical too; when it is time to stand up in the boardroom for the right action, leaders have the courage and clarity to make a call. Leaders often attract followers over a virtuous position established with inner courage.

Even the quietest person can have this quality of courage. A bold stand need not be accompanied by shouting—in fact, the demure person with a compelling idea may be more persuasive than someone who rants. Courage is about the ability to advance in the face of adversity and challenge. When you see someone do this, behold the leader.

## HOW DO I LEARN LEADERSHIP SKILLS

The best way to learn leadership skills is through *doing something that changes peoples' lives*. Leaders make decisions. They take risks, and they feel the pressure of putting their reputation on the line.

In Toastmasters, we elect club officers every six months or annually. The stakes are usually small, yet people care about their Toastmasters experience. Our officers are often new to the experience, reluctant, and someone told them to do it ("volun-told").

The Toastmasters experience represents one of the finest leadership development programs I know.

The military also is well known for building leaders. When I talked to veterans in 2007 about their leadership experiences for my doctoral dissertation, many of them told me, "We had to learn to make life-and-death decisions." These decisions could kill someone—so you learned to do it responsibly.

I recommend that people learning leadership also do these things:

- **Read leadership wisdom.** I recommend Peter Drucker (*The Essential Drucker,* 2001), Jim Kouzes & Barry Posner (*The Leadership Challenge,* 1987), and Warren Bennis (*On Becoming a Leader,* 2009). Reading doesn't automatically make you a leader, but it can help shape you to think like one.
- **Find a mentor.** Talk to someone who has more experience than you, and follow the mentor's guidance. You will accelerate your progress as a leader if someone intelligent and compassionate helps you go through some challenges.
- **Commit to a cause.** Be a leader at something, even if it's a volunteer activity rather than a work one. Make sure your commitment is something that you believe in, and that you are ready to take personal risks in order to advance the cause. Volunteer work can be surprisingly challenging: Volunteers follow because they want to be there, not because they are getting paid.
- **Decide what kind of leader you want to be.** There are lots of choices: Do you want to consult with followers or decide and act quickly? Perhaps you are a quiet leader who prefers to work behind the scenes, influencing the action of others. Some leaders express and expand their vision, weaving a captivating vision while others hammer the parts together. Other leaders are champions at building coalitions dedicated to a unified purpose. Consider creating a leadership journal. Identify leaders admired from television, movies, novels and history, and clarifying why these leaders are worth emulating (or not). Review who you are and what a leader is likely to do in your situation. Realize that you are also free to change your mind at a later date!
- **Hang out with other leaders.** Talk to them about the issues that you face, and listen for the things that they do in

moments of challenge. Discuss their successes with them, and offer realistic service that you can in order to help them get ahead.

Leaders are remarkable for what they can do, by themselves and with other people. We associate a number of qualities and virtues with leaders. Nevertheless, leaders are highly individualistic. They don't resemble each other.

When you climb your Mount Olympus, your capacity to perform will be stretched. You will find that you have new adaptive capacity, the ability to change with circumstances as needed. The climb up the mountain with others will teach any leader how to be flexible in order to bring out the best talent in other people. In creating your success, you will become a changed person, defined by your values, vision and intention. The top of Olympus was the home of the Greek deities. In order to approach such a summit, you will have to transform yourself in preparation.

## DR. STEVE'S TIP

We could study leadership all day, and that would not change a thing. Be confident in what you believe in, and help other people become successful with you. That is the only formula you will need in order to live and work as a leader.

# Chapter 3: What Is Success...and How Do We Achieve It?

*What does success feel like to you?*
*Contentment. ~ Nikki*
*Relief. ~ Lene'*
*A sweet hug. ~ Connie*
*Exhaustion mixed with pride. ~ Joel*
*A sigh of great relief of accomplishment, LIKE YESSS! Followed with a whole lot of respect for the term gratitude as a salute to everyone and everything surrounding me! Very amazing feeling. ~ Chris*
*Success is the exhilaration of having attained a goal, combined with the relief of having completed a job well done. ~ Lisa*
*It feels like the first day in kindergarten. Only, they're telling me about real issues that actually hit home to a lot of folks. The only difference between men and boys being the price of their toys—it feels like success is learning, learning, learning...and some growing. ~ Dana*
*A sense of accomplishment following a challenge. ~ Roy*
*Success is not letting fear win. It's each step we take in the direction of our higher selves, our authentic nature. It's the moments we choose an abundant and victorious perspective rather than one of lack and victimhood. Success often comes in small steps, but can lead to big things! ~ Kristen*
*Making a goal and actually obtaining it! ~ Danette*

Do you pursue success? Does success mean a high-income, sustainable lifestyle for you, or a life surrounded by love, appreciation, good health and music—or something completely different? A successful life does not mean "no work" or "free of labor." For many people, achieving success includes finding work that is agreeable, and compatible with their values. Success leaves us feeling confident.

We may call successful living to be a uniquely different experience for each of us. For some, the journey of finding and pursuing meaningful goals is the experience of success itself—for others, it's a continuous move toward greater achievements. Perhaps we don't recognize success until we pause, look over our lives for the past few years, and gasp with an inner recognition of the journey: "Look at how far I've come!"

Do you want to be more successful than you currently are? Have you climbed one Mt. Olympus, only to recognize that there's another peak in your sights? Perhaps you have read advice on success and leadership, and have made some changes in your life. Have you committed to the practice of a successful life? Many people try out the right behaviors, but fail to continue them until they become sustainable habits.

Whatever changes in your daily life, the best approach is to pick a single new behavior, and live in accord with it. Keep this new way of living close to you, and keep it up for two months before you consider adding another new change to the way you live. Even a single change, if well selected, can lead a person to a more effective way of working and living. Choose the most important behavior that you must adopt in your quest for success. Keep doing it until it is a comfortable, second-nature way of working.

## THOUGHTS ON SUCCESS FOR GREAT THINKERS

What have the world's great thinkers had to say on the topic of success? Let's review a few of the most influential.

### JAMES ALLEN

James Allen, author of *As a Man Thinketh (1903)*, began his life in rather desperate financial circumstances, so he was familiar with the limitations of the world. Drawing inspiration from ancient wisdom—such as the Biblical proverb, "As a man thinketh, so is he"—Allen's philosophy emphasized that people can create their future through the power of intentional and directed thought. While men do not control their circumstances, they can choose their thoughts; thoughts, in turn, will shape circumstances

Allen insists that even in a weakened and desperate state, man is the master of his circumstances. He encourages us to be productive with our efforts, as gold and diamonds are in the fields around us. Countless modern writers on success repeat this theme.

Allen promoted the idea that clear, intentional thought can provide a purpose for the direction of a man's life. By following this purpose, a person might achieve fantastic things. Good health and vitality are influenced by a man's thoughts. A person who pursues great success should crystallize his thinking into a vision. Once developed, a vision is a wonderful thing to comprehend; cherish it. Allen does not merely recommend ambition for the purpose of wealth alone; the final chapter in *As a Man Thinketh* discusses serenity and the attainment of a life of value.

## NAPOLEON HILL

Almost every contemporary success champion who writes or talks about success mentions the contribution of Napoleon Hill, whose *Think and Grow Rich (1937)* remained a best seller for decades. Born in Appalachia less than two decades after the Civil War, Napoleon moved from poverty to financial wealth. He practically defined the contours of the philosophy of the self-help movement in the 20th century, packaged then as a "philosophy of achievement." Hill's focus is directed to financial independence and wealth gaining, which reflects the severity of the economic conditions that he endured; his message, however, need not be limited to a formula for getting rich. Hill taught people that success was theirs to achieve if they would set their minds into the right frame of thinking.

He encouraged all who sought success to develop a friendly alliance with colleagues who hold supportive views. In the *mastermind principle*, Hill advocated that success-seekers should regularly gather to discuss their goals: "Every mind needs friendly contact with other minds, for food of expansion and growth." As Hill and his followers express this concept, when individuals form a mastermind group, the members help each other with ideas, critical thinking, positive support, and finding opportunities for each other.

A mastermind group expands one's chances of having a positive breakthrough and helps a person make intelligent choices.

The mastermind principle is valuable as a stand-alone concept, but it also is part of Hills' 17 Success Principles. He argued that success required developing a "definite major purpose," which provides conviction and certainty, and shapes one's mental attitude. Beginning with thinking, a successful person understands why he or she is moving forward—a starting point for lifelong achievement. Once this purpose is understood and clearly seen, a successful person can apply the mastermind principle to extend the impact in a broader range. Other people can help us achieve the definite major purpose if we are willing to connect and trust with the right people.

Review your definite major purpose regularly. The focus of this gaze, according to Hill, comes to permeate the subconscious mind. After the successful person has decided on this course of action, then the subconscious mind will be working on this issue even while the conscious mind is solving other matters.

Finally, Hill encourages success seekers to apply faith, which helps us take action even when we have no certainty about the outcome. In addition, success seekers with pleasing personalities will help attract people to their cause.

## EARL NIGHTINGALE

Radio personality Earl Nightingale was among the many people influenced by Napoleon Hill. Nightingale promoted the idea that "We become what we think about all the time"—again, an idea drawn from Biblical scripture, but which also resonates with Hill's concept of a definite major purpose.

Nightingale intrigued many success-oriented people with his concept of "the strangest secret." This secret reveals that we are already near the threshold of success, because the secret is "we are what we think about all the time." Hence, if one replaces outmoded thoughts with new thoughts that point us toward success, we are bound to move in that direction. This secret is strange because it shows us that we are already creating our world with our current thoughts, and if one wants to be successful, one needs to take control of one's thinking. Could success simply be as simple as changing, clarifying and expanding one's thinking?

Nightingale developed a useful definition: "Success is the progressive realization of a worthwhile ideal." This definition emphasizes that success is a continual state of becoming. Also consider the identification of a "worthwhile ideal." Success moves a person toward an ideal state. Perhaps that ideal is never fully manifested in the world, yet the person moves closer and closer as he or she applies effort. The success arises from having the ideal, and working toward it.

In Nightingale's view, the ideal is worthwhile which serves the leader well. Positive values are one way to attract followers to the leader's mission. Worthwhile ideals may be adopted by others and become a compass point to guide the achiever during conditions of doubt and tumult.

Nightingale told followers that the mind is like a field, and successful people are like farmers tending to that field. If the mind can take us to success, we must plant the right crops in the field. We may choose to fertilize that field with worthwhile ideals and cultivate that field by our actions. The field will require regular attention, but when attended to regularly, the field will sustain the farmer and his or her family for many years.

The field doesn't care what the farmer plants in it. If the conditions are right, and sufficient attention is placed to its condition, a bountiful harvest of grapes, corn or rice may be returned. Likewise, the mind is capable of generating many different successful outcomes. The successful leader must simply care for that field with a definite purpose.

## BRIAN TRACY

Earl Nightingale emphasized that one must carefully plant the thoughts that will yield a harvest of prosperity and success. Brian Tracy, an entrepreneur, speaker and author came to a similar proposition about success. Tracy asked, "Why are some people successful, and other people are not?" Doesn't it make sense that everyone would reach for success if they could? For Tracy, the difference between successful people and less successful people is what they think about. "Successful people think differently," concluded Tracy.

According to Tracy, successful people not only "plant their fields" with the right seeds of success, they also cultivate self-esteem. They continually support their self-image with positive self-talk. Self-esteem helps keep an achiever working in the right direction. A person with high self-esteem can face rough moments – challenges – and renew their efforts toward their definite purpose. Self-esteem is an internal assessment of one's worth; a person with genuine self-esteem is known to others by his or her smile, tone of voice, and consistent behavior. One cannot fake the real impact of a positive self-esteem; other people seem to be able to look into the inner world and get a "soul reading" of the achiever's self-esteem.

Tracy has talked about a "serendipity principle." If we have self-esteem, if we have a definite purpose, and if we can focus our minds on the target, we are likely to find what we are looking for! Good things come to us by serendipity. The prepared mind knows what it is looking for, and finds that goal with more efficiency and speed than the mind which simply has a desire. By preparing ourselves (high self-esteem) and preparing our mind, an achiever increases the odds that what is being sought will come into one's world. As Tracy tells his followers, "Success doesn't happen to you by watching TV."

What do you think about the "Law of Attraction?" The more I learn, the more I am amazed by the mysteries of life that I don't understand. The ideas discussed by Tracy, Nightingale and other success teachers seem to point in the direction of the Law of Attraction (LOA). In fact, Tracy has taught that we attract into our lives those things that we get emotional about.

I believe that our actions influence the world. Once an action occurs in a system, we can describe the consequences of that act as a ripple. A person of definite action has a verifiable impact; both in physical states and emotional reality.

Actions originate from thoughts. Thoughts are not actions; however thoughts have a profound influence on others. Beginning with thought, leaders can bring people into accord with a common purpose. Thought can inspire and sustain action. Together, thought and action are amplified forces for change when intentionally applied. The person with definite thought and action has a much greater impact than his or her colleague who is still building focus for the purpose.

The law of attraction can be understood by remembering that thought and action together generate a lot of influence. We may never know just how much influence we have created; like George Bailey in It's a Wonderful Life (1946), the impact of our effort is unknown to us. If we were capable of seeing the world from the perspective of angels, we might truly see how we have changed the world. The mystery of attraction works to our advantage when we combine focus of thought and action.

## JIM ROHN

American businessman, author and speaker Jim Rohn also developed a comprehensive theory of success. He wrote about the five components of success that include a personal philosophy, attitude, action, results and lifestyle. Rohn typified the American "rags to riches" story, achieving financial independence and his success by the age of 31.

Rohn recommends that all achievers and leaders build a personal philosophy of life. An intensely practical man, he encourages others to think about how they learn, and especially observe how they make decisions. He argues (like Plato) that the unexamined life is not worth living. Rohn says that we should all reflect on what we feel is failure; we should reflect on what we understand to be a success. A personal philosophy is enhanced by listening to others and by keeping a written journal.

Attitude is the second component of success for Rohn. An achievement-oriented attitude will reflect one's past, and the future will pull the leader. Rohn teaches that an attitude will determine one's potential for future advancement and produces the intensity of our activity. With an attitude as our internal fire, the quality of our results is determined. Attitude sets the quality.

"Weeds will take over your garden," Rohn warned against choosing too much rest. He recognizes that we all need rest; however he taught that the activity should be one's objective. The intelligent leader begins action with an informed choice; choices that reflect the objectives, priorities and attitude of the achiever. Accordingly, Rohn encourages leaders to plan their work. Planning leverages one's time and accelerates results. Rohn thought that planning should be simple, frequent, and demonstrate disciplined action.

Successful people get results. We all get results; however, successful people feel satisfaction from their results. Rohn taught that we could assess our results by what we have, by our use of time, and by what we become. A life well spent demonstrates the values of its foundation. A life built around consistent values will attract success in like kind. Rohn encouraged his followers to increase their value, thereby increasing their results.

The fifth component of Rohn's philosophy of success is lifestyle. Most successful people seek to build a robust lifestyle. The achieved lifestyle, according to Rohn, will reflect one's attitude, activity, and values. A person working consistently over time will earn a platform of enhanced lifestyle benefits. Even small efforts applied consistently can yield impressive results.

## MY SUCCESS INFORMANTS

I spoke with 35 successful people about their success and how leadership helped them reach it. I wanted to reach people from a broad range of life experiences, so I talked to international speakers, nonprofit leaders, high tech entrepreneurs, several physicians, and business executives. My success informants gave me additional insight into the meaning of success which I share with you in the pages that come.

Human experience can teach us a great deal if we pay attention. I decided to focus on a few key questions which can give us all insight into the relationship between leadership and the creation of success. The next chapter will introduce the three big questions that I have focused on for more than two years.

I asked each of my informants "Which book has influenced you the most in becoming successful?" If you would like to see their answers, skip ahead to Appendix II. I have added many of their books to my reading list. You might enjoy reading these books too!

The success informants, in the pages to come, will share their experiences about their travels up Mt. Olympus and help you to create your own ascent to the top. These leaders are qualified to help all of us achieve more with our lives and business. Collectively, their voices may be your guide as you assume your role as a successful leader.

## PUTTING THOUGHT INTO ACTION

I believe that leadership skills can accelerate the journey toward success. Leadership is concerned with both right thought, definite action, and influencing others. Leaders get things done, and a sufficiently developed leader may be able to build a profound transformation for others while ensuring his or her success at the same time.

Leaders take others on a journey of change with them. It is meaningless to talk of a leader working only for his or her personal change. Leaders bring others with them! The best leaders know that others will make a commitment to support the leader's mission if they have trust and involvement with the leader's work. In fact, one of the most interesting outcomes of leadership is that they tend to produce more leaders. A decisive leader can increase opportunities for a number of people around him.

Leaders are just "luckier" at creating success than other people. The work of leaders puts them into situations where they generate more action that moves them into their success zone. One of the most important things that leaders do is to create a large supportive network. Leaders learn how to be persuasive, and many people mentally register to be part of the leader's drive forward.

The supportive network like the leader's values, they like the way that the leader communicates, and they like the hope that the leader shares with others.

Who else can build such a unique support system? While leaders may learn the art of command, their skill at influence is powerful, exceeding the ability to give orders. People willingly join a coalition of positive thought and change that a leader offers their world. The support network of a leader is vitally charged with potential to create change. The leader has the permission of the group to make it happen. See why leaders are often successful?

## DR. STEVE'S TIP

Think about what success means to you. Write it down, and discuss it with someone who you believe is qualified to help you achieve a victory. Listen to people who have achieved a significant success, at least in your eyes. Try doing some of the things that they say.

Don't take success advice from people who you feel are less successful than you — even if you love them. Our friends and family are important to us, but they may not help us transform our lives. Indeed, they may have a personal agenda that works against helping you from change.

Keep loving the important people in your life. Listen to success advice from qualified sources.

# Chapter 4: Three Big Questions

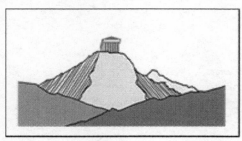

*Questions are the work of the mental explorer.*
*Transformative questions are the hallmark of the leader.*
*The leader of the future is likely to ask more questions than the leader of the past. (See Goldsmith, 1996,* The Leader of the Future.*) The successful person also uses questions, as the work of success involves helping other people get what they want. The process of asking good questions—and diligently seeking the answers—informs the successful person and helps to achieve the desired ends.*

*Be a question asker. Look for the important questions that no one else is asking.*

*What are the essential questions that drive you as you ascend your own personal Mt. Olympus?*

*Take a look at what you want to know. If you are creating a success, then you probably have been focused on questions about happiness, relationships, or making money.*

*In my experience in working toward success, I've learned that finding answers may also generate more questions. In a leadership role, that cycle never ends.*

## DISCOVER THE POWER OF QUESTIONS

Here's a paradox: We all believe that we are free to create our destinies, make our choices, and select the paths to the future. Don't you? Still, when a leader speaks up, we tend to pay attention, and the leader captures our mind's gaze.

Do leaders grab your attention?

I just asked you a question. You may have thought about it for a moment, or had an image of a leader pop into your head. Whether you answered yes or no, I directed you to think about my topic, by a simple query about your opinion.

That's the power of a question. A question unanswered hangs in consciousness, practically pulsating with power, prepared to grab attention. People think they are right; they have all the correct answers, and a question is a challenge to their existence.

If you are free to make your choices, then a question should not be able to influence your direction, right? If I give you an order, you might be compliant (do what I say), ignore it altogether, or go in the opposite direction, depending on your disposition to authority. Leaders may have the power of authority; that authority must be earned for each follower.

Questions are an important tool for the evolved leader. Rather than giving orders, the leader promotes the thinking of the people who follow; carried on long enough, people develop the pattern of thinking of a leader.

This is an ancient concept: The classical Greek philosopher Socrates created a system of education built on the power of questions. Every person arrives at a situation with some knowledge relevant to the challenge. With effective questions, the leader can help students and followers anticipate the possible, and "peer around the corners" of the apparent. Socratic questioning is respectful of the learner and gives credit for arriving at the best solution, with guidance, without command.

Questions are also a two-way street, of course. As I performed the interviews for this book, I heard a number of repeated questions directed *to me*.

## "WHAT ARE YOU DISCOVERING?" "ARE THERE SOME STANDARD ANSWERS? "CAN YOU SUMMARIZE WHAT YOU HAVE LEARNED?"

The challenge was that the information was burying me! I had not yet begun to distill meaningful patterns, because I was still collecting information. I knew that I would find those answers, but I had not yet begun organizing the thematic responses. The benefit was that the interviewees' questions forced me to focus my mind, resulting in these three big questions about my data:

1. What does it mean to be successful?
2. What leadership behaviors help one to be successful?
3. What do leaders do after they stumble?

Once I had these issues in front of me, it became far more meaningful to look through my interview collection. The questions directed me to include some information, and ignore other information. The choice of a few focused questions allowed me to become productive at another level. My work was choosing the most relevant information out of all the interviews in order to answer these questions.

## QUESTIONS DIRECT RESEARCH

A person with a question and a method of answering it is about to start doing research. Research is simply a way of understanding the world, designed to provide information that is verified by data collected and organized to produce meaning. Any worthwhile research project will have a driving question.

Leadership is my passion; it is a complex subject in which people mean different things by that word. How is it possible to learn about leaders and the way they develop, their influence on the world? One method of learning about them is by studying experiences. I enjoy talking to leaders, and I have been able to coax some very interesting conversations out of people who fill that role.

The process led me to gain more information about the world of successful living. Questions are like a lamp in a dark cave; I discover that as I moved forward in my study, the questions forced me to narrow my direction. It's a human impulse to move in many directions—we all like to think we can multi-task!—but the focus of a question draws you into the center of the problem.

Our minds seek closure and the ability to reduce options with a firm answer. If you choose to become a leader, or perhaps a servant of others, you must find the essential questions to allow a sure means of gaining progress. Narrow them down to a few meaningful questions, and let your mind work hard on them.

You may discover knowledge relevant to you, and you may be able to help others with the special knowledge that you have earned through directed inquiry. Chosen correctly, your questions may lead you to becoming a unique and valuable leader for the world.

The development of this book followed a structured, qualitative research process. It was important for me to collect important information that could help real people. The review of interviews from my success informants followed a systematic process. If you would like to see some of the planning and activity that went into my climb up Mt. Olympus with this book, skip ahead to Appendix IV: Collecting Data About Leadership and Success.

## CHANGE YOUR QUESTIONS, CHANGE YOUR LIFE

My life has been given impetus because of an inspiring teacher, Dr. Marilee Adams. Her disarmingly powerful book, *Change Your Questions, Change Your Life* (2009), teaches that there are two modes of operating in this world: judger and learner.

There are some advantages to both working modes. The learner is a person who proceeds by asking intelligent questions, trying to understand as much as possible. Judgers are fast to act, having made up their minds, and disliking time in doubt. The judger is certain of almost anything.

Judging mode is convenient and fast. Learning mode means asking questions and patiently encouraging others to contribute their best work. Judging works when it's time to give orders. Learning builds relationships.

Both roles have a place in a leader's repertoire—the trick is to know when to use the appropriate mode.

Don't look to me to be perfect! I strive to be a learner, but I slip into my judger role rather quickly, and I am not always aware of the transition until later. I was recently in a conversation with a family member, and I jumped into my judger persona quickly—almost as if my personality had been hijacked! I blamed, I vented, and I raised my voice. It was terrible, and luckily the episode was over quickly.

The best leaders need to treat people well. A patient leader who is a learner most of the time helps to cultivate the people who work for him. A learner will ask questions—and can still guide people (through awareness and discovery) to better ways of working.

## GREAT LEADERS HAVE INQUIRING MINDS

Let's face it: Some people enjoy telling other people what to do, while others prefer to ask. Both can achieve similar ends. Don't forget that asking can include the practice of asking other people for their involvement—in a very real way, they are the sherpas in your Mt. Olympus journey!

The best leaders ask questions, and work much of the time in learner mode. Leaders and learners want to know what is going on. The leader with an inquiring mind can get more than data—people surrounding them may also have impressions, emotional reactions, and intuitive guesses about the nature of their work environment. Great leaders want to gain information from their followers.

An effective leader will probe for those critical impressions. The skillful use of the question moves the center of power away from the leader, and into the hands of the person sharing information. The paradox of great leadership is that leaders don't need a lot of power! They are interested in building the strength and effectiveness of the people around them. Once followers understand the nature of the leader's support, they become deeply loyal. When the leader and follower are in alignment, the leader does not need to wield power in the traditional sense.

Power is often shifted into the hands of members, especially when the followers have current frontline experience that the boss does not have. The effective leader encourages the voices of others and helps them to become responsive to the needs of their work. Nevertheless, the process of asking questions keeps a different kind of power in the hands of the leader: They become agents aligned with his purpose.

The inquiring mind of the leader recognizes that other people can contribute substantially to the development of policy and to the implementation of the vision. Through questions, the leader helps to reveal the core values that structure the nature of work. Leaders develop other people's potential by asking them to consider possibilities and consequences.

## QUESTIONS SPUR INTELLECTUAL AND MORAL DEVELOPMENT

Questions also help leaders to grow into their roles, by forcing their minds and nervous systems to adapt—and at a smaller cost than learning from painful experience.

Scholar and organizational consultant Warren Bennis has written extensively about the transformative power of crucible experiences. Without doubt, all leaders face life and career challenges which transform them through hard decisions applied to critical business choices. In metallurgy, a crucible is a superheated container that melts a metal so that it now takes a new form, perhaps in creating an alloy that takes on qualities of new ingredients. Leaders are like this too: Some experiences create unforgettable heated moments that melt the leader into a new form, one that may have new qualities—perhaps wiser, more flexible, stronger, and more resistant to heat in the future.

Questions force the leader to enter the crucible without taking as much heat. An intelligent leader will anticipate the great transformation that follows the melting process. The mind and conscience become experienced by the process of preparing for change. A good question challenges the mind to anticipate consequences and places the decision-maker at choice point!

Intelligent people have access to large amounts of information. Nevertheless, the experience of acting and deciding in the face of confusion and turmoil can be limited. Even smart, well-informed people will not always know what to do.

Leaders will be called to anticipate a variety of factors: What do people need to know? How do you connect people in a crisis? How do you maintain confidence while the storm of confusion is breaking around you? Leaders are called to make decisions under less-than-optimal circumstances, and help those around them feel stronger just at that moment.

The questions of leadership prepare the mind and conscience for action. We tend to judge leaders by their actions: What did they do, and were their people ready to act? Well-designed questions further the process of transformation, as do hard moments of conflict and uncertainty.

Let's dig deeper. Expanding the three questions mentioned earlier in this chapter may reveal greater value for leaders and success-seekers:

1. **What does success mean**? Is success a strictly personal experience, or does it involve other people? Can a leader help other people become successful? What else does success mean besides financial gain and the accumulation of power?
2. **What are the leadership behaviors that support success**? Can we act as a leader and increase our chances of being successful? How should we help other people? Is a personal success possible without helping others? How can we get better at making these leadership decisions?
3. **What do leaders do after they stumble**? How do leaders act after they have had an intense negative experience? What can one do to remain resilient?

Ask yourself how your thinking compares with leaders and successful people. Do you have a clear image of what your success looks like? Consider responding as a leader for the challenges that you will face.

## SUCCESS: WE MAY NOT BE TALKING ABOUT THE SAME THING

We don't consult dictionaries as we speak, so the definition of success may vary between different people. We use the same words; do we mean the same things? When we look at the uses of words—a deep linguistic exercise—that's when real communication is taking place.

I once heard a speaker talk about money and how his audience proved to him that they intended different things even by that one word. What was remarkable about this speaker's experiment was that he was speaking to a group of accountants. Isn't that amazing? One would think that a profession dedicated to the measure and control of money should only have a superficial disagreement on such a point. Yet, money could mean the paper folded in my wallet or expected revenues from a new product launch. It could mean a chance to take a friend out on a date or the assignment of value for the budget next quarter. On a tropical island, money might also mean shells used in barter.

Success, too, is a concept open to multiple interpretations. (See chapter 6 for a discussion of this topic.) Are you willing to expand what you believe about success? Adopting a leader's perspective will require it.

## LEADERSHIP BEHAVIORS: A LINK TO SUCCESS

If you could do one thing differently to be more successful, what would it be? In my own business, for example, I have decided that I need to speak to more people. More specifically, I must ask more people if they want my services as an executive coach.

Why is it that certain behaviors can make us successful?

Philosophically, I operate under the assumption that we are closer than we realize to the success we envision. All we need to do is tweak a few—maybe only one—critical behavior. If I do something different or new, I will have a success breakthrough.

What are the right leadership behaviors to examine? There are many to consider; for most of us, a breakthrough to better leadership will not come in the ways we often believe, such as better time management or less effort wasted on personal social media.

John Maxwell, in his book *The Five Levels of Leadership* (2013), describes the evolutionary growth of a leader. A caterpillar has many qualities different from the more mature form of a butterfly. So, too, if we talk about a beginner, level-one leader, the behaviors may be substantially different than an expert level-five leader at the helm of a Fortune 500 conglomerate.

It can get confusing to find the *best leadership behaviors* that promote success. Fortunately, we have a reliable source: The opinions and experiences of successful people, those who've already summited Mt. Olympus. Their views suggest to us a preferred group of behaviors that will help one be successful.

## WHAT DOES IT MEAN TO STUMBLE?

> *Success is stumbling from failure to failure with no loss of enthusiasm.*
> ~ *Winston Churchill*

Everyone stumbles. Many of the people I interviewed for this book said something like, "I stumble every day."

Experiencing an upset in plans, however, does not mean that the game is over. It just means that things did not go perfectly.

I don't know about you, but I find that reassuring. I stumble more often than I like to admit. The mark of a successful person is the ability to pick up and move forward in a positive way, after falling flat. Take time to address the wounds, but don't stay down! Refocus yourself on the journey, and recognize that the occasional slowdown is part of success.

I'd also suggest that, when you see someone else stumbling, reframe your mindset: "Here is a future leader. Here is a success. What can I do to be a ray of light to that person?" After all, you've fallen too haven't you?

## MY OWN BIG STUMBLE: HOW LEADERSHIP HELPED

I remember all-too-vividly being fired in January 1990. I thought it was unfair, but it wasn't unexpected. I had helped to sell my family business to a company that operated child-care centers, coast-to-coast, and I'd done my best make the company as valuable as it could be. I trained directors, and put my heart into it. I made sure our buildings looked excellent, that our classrooms were well-stocked. I cultivated great relationships with people who worked several levels below my managers. In addition, I looked forward to helping make the child-care business excellent after the sale. I thought I would work for the purchasing corporation—after all, they needed to run the business they had bought. Instead, I was asked to leave. I'll never forget the words of man who fired me, he said, "Steve, don't take this personally." Really? I'd cared a lot about the business, devoted my life to making it excellent—I really had! Now I had to walk away? It sure felt personal.

It was very hard looking for work. I moved from the top chair in the company to working the street, and very few people understood what it meant to me. Those who did understand were still working in the business. It was an emotionally rocky phase of my life. I felt like the parade of life and career had picked up a triumphant baton and marched right on by me. Some days I moved forward with the confidence that new work was right ahead of me. On other days, I felt massive despair.

What I have since learned is that just about everyone has dark periods like this. Progress is still possible even though your emotions move through a roller-coaster ride—up, down, sideways, and barrel rolls. Nevertheless, leaders must move forward: plan intelligently, manage time and energy, and continue to expand professional networks. Circumstances always change, and fortune comes to the prepared mind.

## THE LEADER'S SECRET: COURAGE

Reading the work of existential psychologist Rollo May taught me that courage is an enabling value. With courage, I will go to places previously unexplored; I will take appropriate risks, and importantly, my sights will be looking ahead. The courageous leader is willing to move beyond conformity and ask, "I like what I see up there on Mt. Olympus. What will it take for me to charge up there?" Vision is that sense of having the courage to affirm the possible future and to decide, "I'm going to take others with me. That is where I am going."

I worked for 30 years in my family business. I was very comfortable, but could not take the risks to move the business where I wanted; I was a player, but not the owner. I could afford to have a vision to do something new, because my assets were not at risk.

With my family business mostly dissolved, I realized that there was no safety in thinking securely. Having the courage to think ahead is the safest position for me, I thought; without it, I might end up working in a dead-end job far below my aspirations. Courage has become my friend, and vision has become my practice.

I have been pushed forward—by necessity—into living courageously. I love it—and worry that I might find a comfort level too soon. I have come to understand the words of the American billionaire Larry Ellison, who noted that every day all his wealth, his entire organization could crumble. His strength came from knowing how to live courageously and taking steps never to be complacent. For as one enjoys one's rewards prematurely, the need to act with courage may decline in urgency.

May tells us that courage "gives reality to all other virtues and personal values." When we live courageously, we advocate what is important to us. The courageous person lives by his or her values with a minimum of compromise.

Find a person with a vision, add courage, and a path to an inspired future, and you've got a champion who will move the frontier of the possible forward. Courage is necessary because leaders will encounter ardent resistance—either vigorous and obvious, or below the surface, unannounced—as they move the vision forward. Courage helps to face the unexpected, in recognition that one's strength will be sufficient to meet the challenges.

## DR. STEVE'S TIP

Where can you find the questions that will help you in your leadership and success journey? I suggest that you begin by exploring your journey forward. Start asking questions, and through an iterative process, you may discover the questions that hold the greatest value for you in your travel up Mt. Olympus.

**Ask questions about what you need to learn.** I want to be a better negotiator. I also want to be the best salesperson in the world for project managers. Knowing that I can learn more, I am always asking myself how I can improve my work in these areas. What do you need to learn?

**Ask questions about how you can help your customers better.** Put a great deal of attention on the people for whom you are working. Understand the psychology of your clients, and seek to understand their motivations. Pay attention to your customers' dreams, and find a way to earn their trust.

**Ask questions about how you can do your work faster and with greater efficiency.** Always be looking for ways to get your work done with greater ease and less cost. Look at your business and professional practice as a set of processes; what steps may no longer be necessary? Look frequently and ask hard questions.

**Ask questions about the people you need to meet.** Some people may help you as a gateway to further success. In turn, you might be able to help these people. Be looking for these people, and ask questions, such as "How can I be helpful to this person?" or "Who will help me meet this person?"

# Chapter 5: The Three Categories of Success

*Just as you are unique, your experience of success will be unique to you. Your struggle to get to the top of Mount Olympus will create moments that you will remember the rest of your life. These moments will inform the way you work as a leader of men and women. No one else can claim the same struggle and moment of victory as you have. Accordingly, what you say about success will be highly personal and reflect your challenge, your struggle.*

*Mount Olympus is different for all of us.*

*Do think about what being successful means to you. There are paradoxes here for you: Many people do not feel successful unless they are making a difference for the people around them. For many of us, success comes from serving others. It is time to think about what you must do in order to feel successful.*

*Don't copy someone else's version of success, because you may discover, "This isn't as good as I thought it would be." No one will give you success either. It will be something you invite into your life.*

Onward to success!

Certain conditions may hint at success—happiness, financial achievement, sustainability, sharing it with others—but they don't necessarily identify what success means to the person who has achieved it. Success isn't a lottery ticket: Common sense and experience show us that a success must be earned by preparatory work.

Leadership behaviors and values can push a personal success to a higher level. Leaders change the world of people around them. Great success is a shared experience; leaders bring others along with them. Success isn't generally a solo act.

As the people in my interviews confirmed their achievements and spoke about the meaning of success, I found that success fell into the three primary categories discussed below. Do these fit your own experience? If yes, what are you doing to cultivate the necessary behaviors and actions? If not, what does success mean to you…and how do you plan to get there?

## SUCCESS IS THE EXPERIENCE OF REACHING A GOAL

Getting hired for a great job, completing a college degree, or winning a competitive race are some of the images that might pop into your head when thinking about success. We'll see hats thrown in the air, Gatorade poured on the winning coach, or boisterous shouting. It is fun and memorable to reach a goal, and the experience of fulfillment can last a long time.

Think back on the last time you earned a big goal. Was it something that you worked on for a long time? Did you ever doubt you could make it to the finish line? When you finally made it, what did it feel like?

If your goal is to sing on Broadway, the action steps might include taking vocal lessons, applying for auditions, and learning the trade of show business. As you move closer to fulfilling your goal, your internal "success-feeling monitor" starts to soar. Once my goal is achieved I probably add another goal—perhaps to sing on four continents, or to record a best-selling album.

I'm not a Grammy-caliber singer, but I experienced the goal-success process during three particular moments during the past few years. First of all, I earned my black belt in the Japanese martial art of aikido after having studied for 10 years. Yes, 10 years! I remember having pizza and celebrating with friends. I felt fit and loose. I felt the journey wasn't over; I was going somewhere.

I felt a similar state of elation after earning my doctorate, which took five years—including two final years of serious mental doubt over my ability to reach the goal line. My dissertation was turned down twice, and I lost two out of three committee members. I felt very alone, but at least my wife was with me. When I finally made it, I just felt this intense mental clarity and deep satisfaction.

The third example was being awarded a contract to operate a charter school system in Arizona. I had worked on this contract for nearly two years, and doubts were part of the journey. When I did receive the approval to operate, I saw all kinds of possibilities for the future of my charter school organization.

When success is about meeting goals, there's typically a "goal horizon" that moves forward. You achieve one goal, feel great about it, and define a new goal that is a natural extension of the first goal.

A big part of the thrill of achievement comes from making wild, audacious goals happen. Entrepreneur Terry started a Mexican restaurant business with his wife. They loved treating the employees and customers like family. Terry's business is so successful that he opened four locations in five years of work.

Stacey launched a social media company with her brother. They rapidly escalated the size of the business, and sold their mutual interests within three years of launch, making them millionaires. Stacey appeared on the cover of *Seventeen Magazine* by the age of 20.

Some goals become part of our lifelong narrative. We know that we enhance our future possibilities—forever—when we cross the goal line. Success is surely more than the score itself, but those big goals give something to cheer for.

## SUCCESS IS ABOUT HELPING OTHER PEOPLE

Robert, a lawyer and professional speaker, told me, "I feel successful when I know I've helped another person that day." Success is not just about what you have done, but also touching the lives of others and leaving them with additional blessings of life.

In this category, success is not simply about you—it includes an entire success radius, making a larger impact on the world, creating community, or providing wisdom and resources to others. From this viewpoint, success is outward looking; and a better world means that everyone has more abundance. If I have helped others, they will recommend me.

How far can success spread? When you do well, does it touch two, three or more levels of interpersonal connections? Take LinkedIn, for example. I can find the people who know the people who know me; i.e., second-level connections. The people who know them, but don't know me, are third-level connections. You might have hundreds of thousands of people who are only one handshake distant from you right now—just on LinkedIn alone!

Imagine what can happen when you share a positive outlook and help your immediate connections, followed by them influencing the people that they know as well. A person of influence can start a ripple of positivity that could circle the globe. That's the power of the success radius.

Susan told me, "I want my clients to be successful. If that happens to them, they will write testimonial letters for me."

Do you know people who make others successful around them? The beautiful part of this effort is that these people are likely doing well for themselves. Their work changes lives, hence people admire them. Successful people often seek out ways to help the people they care about, and most do not hesitate to ask for help for themselves when needed.

Finding ways to help other people means stretching your talents. The work needed to help other people makes you more capable than when you started out—and this added capability helps you reach your goals.

In essence, you're practicing for coming achievements. New skills—unexpected challenges, unreasonable deadlines, and higher performance standards—may be part of the pressure that comes from helping others. As a benefit, however, you're better prepared for future challenges. The successful giver is simply ready to move forward in expanded ways not known at the start of the journey.

Helping other people is good karma. The person who helps others earns a reputation for it, and may have a growing number of personal advocates who want them to succeed in a major way. A cheering section is nice—though sometimes embarrassing. In a very real way, the successful leader creates independent public relations agents, because people regularly look for ways to return the favor.

"What defines worthwhile obviously depends on somebody's value, but to me a worthwhile goal is one that is not selfish and helps other people," Kirk said. "Preach to the better good of the whole community, and all of the people involved…We are always trying to help them benefit from what we are doing, and as long as we accomplish something that is worthwhile, we could consider ourselves successful."

Successful people often are simply thinking about the well being of other people. They have less need to worry about the details of creating their success.

## SUCCESS IS ABOUT BECOMING MORE SKILLFUL

For many people, success is an expansive experience—creating the ability to take on additional opportunities or the confidence to do progressively daring things. A pilot might seek the skills and license to fly a bigger plane, a jet, or a helicopter—or maybe to crack the sound barrier. The skill challenge can always move forward. Perhaps not surprisingly, one of the common themes from my interview respondents was the ability to accomplish more than they did in the past.

I am actively working on speaking the French language, completing daily assignments, and looking for opportunities to speak French. I don't claim to be fluent—but I believe I can get there. One success condition for my life will be to converse freely and easily in French. Someday, I'd like to do the same in Japanese.

Many professions require continuing education (CE) credits in order to maintain a license to operate. In the real estate profession, the next step is to earn the right to teach a CE course. To do so demonstrates mastery of the material, demonstrated skill at training and public speaking, and a certain amount of political connection as well.

In addition to earning CE credits, some attorneys cultivate expertise that might launch a political career, give them the chance to serve as a judge, lead them to specialize in a particular branch of the law, or to combine legal training with work in another profession.

By working hard in a specialized area, a professional may feel a sense of satisfaction, delight, and empowerment in doing new things. Do you have a skill or new potential that you are working on? Perhaps you, too, will feel successful as you add talent and capability to what you do.

> "I feel like I am doing what I am supposed to be doing, using all my natural skills and filling in the holes with other people who have the skills that I don't have."—Michelle
> "Personal success is for me being able to maintain successfully and grow this business—while at the same time, accomplishing all the things I want to be, accomplishing my personal life in terms of spending time with family or my quality of life at home."—Chris
> "There is a huge group here and there is this other level that is not that far away, but is incrementally different for most to get up to. I've been amazed throughout my career how so many people go up to an 80% level or so and get comfortable, and how much difference every incremental percent past that makes a difference in your success."—Clark

Interestingly enough, no one in my respondent group mentioned "financial independence" as a complete and fulfilling state of success. Financial goals are not enough. It appears that the success is about the internal state, an assessment about one's worth to the world. In short, people feel successful by *meeting goals, helping other people,* and *by becoming more talented and skillful.* An internal state of mind may be more important to a successful person than does the size of the bank account.

## SEEKING THAT MOMENT OF SUCCESS

When have you felt most successful? Think back to a moment or two when your confidence was at an all-time high—when your nervous system said, "You are awesome! You are incredible!"

Let that moment flow through your body, like a wave that spreads a healing energy over every point of your existence. Think of this moment as a spotlight in your life. This moment of success can reveal to you the emotional payoff of achieving something worthwhile—like a beacon that leads you to a better life.

In those moments, your mind was clear of worry. Now, it's time to take that feeling and apply it to a future goal. Visualize your future success, while thinking about of the feeling of a past victory. Hold them together, and work to make it happen.

Make this memory special. Your experience of success can serve you as a transformational ingredient in your professional and personal growth. Expand and be successful—apply a visualization that will help take you there. Show your nervous system that your success is something you have already experienced.

## CHOOSING THE BIG GOALS FOR LIFE

Think about your goals. Successful people give their goals considerable thought. Do you set aside a routine of reviewing your goals, and looking for ways to take action on them? Do you actually take action?

Little goals do not move our hearts. They're achievable, but do not evoke inspiration.

Big goals require courage. Want to feel really successful? Choose a goal that you're not sure you can attain, but one that other people around you have earned.

Leaders often use the term stretch goals. There should be some extraordinary effort in order to make the goal work. The completion of the goal should not be automatic; a goal seeker will not feel successful if the work is ordinary.

Think about this feeling of stretching, this feeling of being successful, which feeds self-confidence. If you have earned enough experience completing goals, then you will have this feeling within you. Relish this feeling. This elation at being successful can help you achieve more.

For example, do you feel any doubts about future challenges? If you don't, you are probably not challenging yourself sufficiently! Look at a specific goal that you currently consider a stretch. Understand you have the talent and skill within you to reach the goal line—but you may have to work hard for it, even harder than you'd prefer.

Here's your secret to boosting your performance: recall that moment where you felt successful in completing a goal. Savor that moment. Swim in it...let your nervous system take in that magic that comes from feeling elation at succeeding. Return with that feeling to your future challenge. Let that positive emotion wash over the challenge that you face. Understand that the confidence you have earned in the past can be earned again on a new challenge.

You are bigger than your goals. You have a huge capacity to achieve great things. Feel your nervous system without experience of success that you have already earned and apply it to future challenges. You will simply be amazing.

## LOOK AHEAD: THE JOURNEY TO LEAD AND INFLUENCE OTHERS

Your big journey is just a potential experience until you decide, and move. Leaders take action. Successful people feel the gift of gladness that they have started. Do you want to begin this journey?

I don't believe life is about the destination. Either we are growing and changing, or we are dying. Life is an evolution, one in which we change and gain new capacity to perform.

We have many potential lives and careers within us. We must use our visionary power if we want them to be realized in the world. Do you see your potential paths ahead of you? You cannot choose them all. You can, however, choose to bring other people with you—this is the leader's option.

Everyone has leadership potential. Leadership skills give us the ability to do more. If I am a skilled painter, leadership skills can enhance what I can do. If I am a soccer player, I will be a better soccer player if I lead on the field. If I am an author, my leadership skills can help influence other people. If I am a jazz musician, I may be able to lead my band to greatness.

Leadership skills can either enhance what we do or put a cap on our ability to do more.

A person with low-level leadership skills will never be a master in the field, because a big part of mastery is about influencing other people to do their best. Leadership skills are worth learning! Leadership skills can help us be successful.

Here is what I have learned: As I make choices, I command my actions and reserve my time, which makes my heart feel right and gives me courage when I work through areas of confusion and doubt. The potential future becomes clearer to me than the start of my journey, and I gain strength.

I believe strongly that there is a potential journey of life for you. Look within, and discover your purpose. Build your leadership skills, and become better at what you do. Influence others to follow a righteous path. I don't know what lies ahead for you, but don't hold on to the habits and choices of the past. Choose the future, and become exquisite at your strengths. Your talents, perhaps hidden within, will surely leave a mark on the world. I believe in you.

## DR. STEVE'S TIP

Earl Nightingale is famous for teaching that the strangest secret is that we become what we think about all the time. Have you chosen a form of success for yourself? Then be aware of your thoughts, and cultivate your form of success. Your mind is a transformational vessel. You have the power to change the way you live your life, to experience more of the things that bring gladness to you, and to bring other people along with you on that journey. If Nightingale is right, the power of your mind hastens this journey. Thoughts of your success, and what you will make of it, change the way you live and determine your actions.

In this chapter, we've discussed several versions of success. Which one is yours? Perhaps you want some of each type.

Do you want to reach goals? Success may be found in the achievement of a number of wins. Ask yourself where you will be when a number of goals have been accomplished. Think about who you are, and how you will help people.

Do you want to help people? Consider being a leader in your work and training other leaders to carry on after you.

Do you want to become more skillful, adding new talents to your repertoire? You will feel exhilarated as you achieve more. How will you use your success and talents to make an impact on the world? Think about extending your talents, working as a leader to do good all around you.

Use the power of your mind to create your version of success — and then do what you can to make things better for other people.

# Chapter 6: What Leaders Do To Be Successful

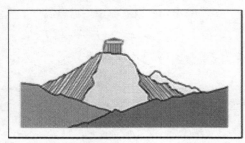

*Leaders are formed by exposure to great ideas, serving people, and making good situations out of negative ones. While some believe the leadership opportunity must be experienced (i.e., leaders are made, not born), others might point to leadership "naturals" in our world, who take the helm by inherent instinct.*

*Not everyone is born to play championship tennis; we can all improve if we have the right experiences. Yet, the best players in the world may have been born with an innate capacity for the sport that they use well.*

*Would you be a leader in your work?*

*There are some experiences that you won't be able to avoid. These may be painful yet may serve you by developing your character and mental power. You can follow the experiences of past leaders; we can learn from people who have gone before us. When needed, we must stand up for ourselves as a leader. We can and should use the gifts that came to us at birth; without doubt we will need to continue growing even beyond our inherent nature.*

*Be ready for an adventure, because that's what a Mt. Olympus journey is.*

Search Google for "top ten leadership qualities," and you'll discover page after page of lists are available to the curious reader. Simply compiling lists—and even acting on them—does not make one a leader, however. Because leaders do different kinds of things, a person who conscientiously models leadership may improve their command image; doing this, though, is not likely going to change the way one connects with people.

Having a purpose and vision is more important than a checklist of model behaviors. A leader becomes memorable when people know why he or she acts. Purpose and vision attract others to join our cause.

Not everyone will agree on how a leader will act, because there are individual differences. Successful leaders have some commonalities, as can be seen from the top behaviors that I recorded from my interviews for this book. If you want to be successful, too, try doing these things.

## SUCCESS BEHAVIOR #1: BELIEVE IN YOUR DECISIONS

This was the most common success trait cited by my interviewees: Leaders believe in what they do, and have an internal consistency in how they act. A good leader is like an evangelist, able to enlist others in their mission.

Believing in one's decisions will bolster confidence. Leaders and successful people don't just make decisions and commit resources; when they act, they display their level of confidence in what they are doing. Remember John Kennedy challenging the United States to send a manned mission to the moon? Even though our best engineers and aviation industry did not know how to do this, even though computer science was in a toddler stage of development, Kennedy acted with the belief that manned spaceflight was possible and necessary. Another American president announced that manned flights to the moon and beyond were going to happen (look up *Vision for Space Exploration*, George Bush, 2004). Bush just did not act as if he believed in his choice. Belief makes a big difference in achieving success and other significant challenges.

Susan, a speaker and business consultant, told me that it was vital to her success to be able to speak to other leaders and convince them of what she was doing.

> I think my ability to speak my opinion in many leadership positions I've been in, on boards of directors, president of organizations, I find that people will sit back and accept the status quo. I find that people will also sit back because they are afraid of controversy.

Not only must leaders believe in what they're doing, they need to speak up in the face of conflict. The successful person will have to convince others that the message is important enough that it survive publicly, in the face of controversy. Successful people become an advocate for their belief.

Jack, a serial entrepreneur, told me that his belief was necessary because so many people doubted him.

I have had people who asked me, "Weren't you worried about losing everything?" And I said, "I never thought of that." The only thing that was on my mind was, *What is the next step? And the next step, and the next step, and the next step, without looking backwards.* Things got done, things got where I wanted to go.

Jack demonstrates the intensity of his belief by eliminating worry from his mind; instead, he focused on the direction forward. He placed his energy into the present and future. He had confidence in his abilities. The leader should focus on the destination and the choices that will take him or her there.
Another man, Suga, spoke of the role of faith.

Definitely faith. I would say faith, the belief in yourself, the belief in dreams you are accomplishing and living your dreams. I think that quality alone, because with that faith, your hope, your love is there, the creativity will come, your determination of course. To me, it's been faith.

This leader is an educator and mentor; he dedicates his life to working with parents who have lost loved ones due to murder and suicide. Through faith, he has the belief he needs to continue, even when individual encounters are discouraging at times—he has the unrelenting belief that he can make a difference for others.

**How does belief create success?** Belief changes the mind. Everyone has logical and emotional components to their thinking. When a person maintains a belief and considers it as a life influence, it strengthens many neurological connections in the brain. We can reinforce our beliefs. A view held, reviewed, and held up to the changing circumstances of life will become a deeper influence on a person than a newly adopted idea.

Have you ever talked to someone who had deeply held beliefs? I don't mean religious proselytizing or network marketing, but someone who is genuinely passionate about the law, military service, music, or art? When you talk to such a person, you can detect that there is a lot under the surface. The person doesn't even have to say too much—but you know that there is a lot there, and you respect that.

A successful person builds a coherent belief system that guides his or her life. Over time, that knowledge will have influenced many decisions, so that when you meet this person on the road to success, you can see where grooves have been worn into their life. Belief like this becomes unstoppable. Other people come to accept the certainty and determination of an individual. When someone is on the trail to Mt. Olympus, others can sense it.

**How do leaders create believing followers?** If there were a super-power connected with leadership, it might involve creating dedicated, believing followers. Some leaders have an extraordinary talent for creating new believers—Apple founder Steve Jobs comes to mind. All leaders must talk to supporters and share their vision in order to get started. People want to know "what's in it for them?" A powerful belief system will examine the past and how it worked at a previous time, and then offer hope about the direction of the future. Leaders believe that they can create their future, and as they attract followers and build a coalition, it becomes easier to make that brighter future happen.

The leaders who do the best job of attracting followers are credible, appreciative, and inclusive. A credible leader can share new belief ideas, and because of what he or she has gone through, those beliefs have a high degree of persuasive value. An entrepreneur who has already built a $10 million company will be highly credible to a new investor when presenting a new business plan. Followers look for signs of credibility as well.

By appreciation, I mean that leaders treat followers as unique, showing how the opportunity to move to success is extended to them as well. Appreciation suggests that followers can be unique and different while holding similar values and beliefs. Great leaders perceive followers as unique people and find ways to appreciate their differences and strengths. Great leaders become successful because of their capacity to believe in others for their unique strengths.

Leaders include followers. The leader on the route to success gives the follower a chance to be meaningfully involved. A leader who includes others opens the door to commitment and belief.

Profound belief not only attracts followers, it also hastens individual and organizational success.

## SUCCESS BEHAVIOR #2: CREATE A TEAM

This behavior was the second most frequently mentioned leadership activity by the respondents in my group of contacts. Teams indicate commitment and shared purpose. Corporate organizations spawn teams, but a group of entrepreneurs can also team together for shared benefit. A team is much more than a group of people with a common interest; in a team, members often have specialized roles and a high level of communication. Members of a group may have a common interest, but this does not necessarily mean they will support their colleagues when sudden challenges arise. In contrast, team members realize that there is a common benefit of reaching a goal together.

Terry, a restaurateur, emphasized how important it is to build a team feeling in his restaurants.

> [Success and leadership is about] working together. This is a team setting. It's a family setting. I've worked in restaurants where there is a division between the back of the house, which would be the kitchen, and the front of the house, which would be the service staff. We've broken down those barriers and kept it where everybody works together. In the past five years, there's not been a battle back and forth over the ball, because people work together. They're willing to do whatever it takes to help out the other individual. That team system, that family system, is really important.

In his restaurants, he conveys the feeling that the restaurant is actually a family party where the customer is invited in as a special guest.

> I want the experience of our guest at 8:59 p.m., the minute before we close, to be the same experience they'd have at 11:30 a.m., when we are super busy. I want them to get a great product no matter what part of the day they are coming in. I want them to be treated as our guests. If a guest walks in at 9:15, we want our staff to say "Sorry, we're closed and the grill is shut down, but we have chips and salsa," or "I can still do bean and cheese burritos, the beans are hot." We can't just say, "We're closed, try us again tomorrow."

Stacey, a young entrepreneur in social media, also emphasized the importance of leading a team well.

> Leadership skill, in terms of hiring the right team, is super important, so communicating with those people before you

> hire them, setting up expectations, [and working] to get those people on the team...

These conditions help to create conditions of success. A team that works well, with clear expectations, supports the achievement of success. Stacey also observed that conditions in the start-up phase of the business can place significant demands on the team.

> To really go through these late nights that a lot of startups do, to keep working to finish features, inspiration needs to be there, communication needs to be there, [and] a positive attitude needs to be there. All of those things come together to make someone successful, and to make a team successful.

Ronnie remembered how important her relationship was with her team during a period of upheaval in her publishing career.

> I was the managing editor and the publications director. I built that product line. Towards the end of those 15 years, the organization determined correctly that publication on drug information, was it really their core competencies. So they put our entire drug information product line on the market and imposed a hiring freeze on my department. This made good sense, because we were all going to be out of work eventually and we knew it.
>
> In September of that year, we all got pink slips and we were told that we had till the beginning of January to finish our production, to produce these thousands of pages. Then we had from January to the end of June to teach the buyout company everything we did and how to do it.
>
> So that it would be a total dump of all of our work. This was me and everyone on my staff. We were told that we would have very good severance packages. You know I sat down with my staff, who were all looking at me with frowning faces and great big grumbles: "What do they think we are, they are supposed to celebrate when we all know our last day of work is June 30."

I looked at them and I said, "Well, I can tell you what to do. I'm going to be out of a job, just like all of you. I will tell you what I always tell you. You need to do what's right for you. What I can tell you is I will tell you what I am going to do and you can make up your mind anyway you want. I've been here almost 15 years. We built this product line and we are all very proud of what we do. I am going to make sure that the production gets done as close to on time as possible; that's really going to depend a lot on all of you. They have paid a lot of money for what we have accomplished, and I want to leave knowing that I have left it as much in good hands as I can, so that I can be proud of what we've done and move on to something even better."

What do you think my staff did? Every single one of them stayed. Not only did we meet the deadline, we came in 25% under budget so that the company gave us all merit bonuses in January.

Those that wanted to seek positions with the buyout company told me, and I helped them any way that I could. Two of them took positions with the buyout company, which is in Denver, and they happily moved there.

I was so pleased and I am still in touch with some of these people. I tell people all the time never burn your bridges. You don't know how long you are going to be in that job, you don't know how long you are going to know the people.

You will find that your team members are the best assets that you could possibly have to make you a good manager.

James, an author and entrepreneur, also spoke about the importance of building teams for leaders.

I view my primary role to use whatever influence and tools I have to develop the leadership capacity of others. Leaders strive to serve and make clear who they are serving at every moment. If one does that, the rest all begins to fall into place. Ideally, in a big organization and enterprise effort, it becomes part of the culture so that everybody is advancing at every moment.

Terry spoke about creating a family feeling at his workplace—teams are like family at his restaurants. Ronnie demonstrated how a leader inspires a team during moments of upheaval, giving all team members a reason to do their best work even while their jobs were slated to be phased out. James points out that leaders build the leadership talent in the people who work for them. The work of a leader supports the work of a team by creating a culture in which people come to expect a definite quality of the relationship with the person in charge. That culture may come to resemble a family or a leadership training academy, and there will be other variations. The culture depends on the guidance of a leader. Leaders show people that they care what happens to them and that their workplace will be more than a set of job functions—people can build meaningful relationships.

Why do successful people build teams? Because a success is not just about an inner state, it involves social relations. Successful people do not work alone. Teams are one of the best organizing principles to achieve a lofty vision.

A team is a focused group of persons who have a shared purpose. The success envisioned by a leader can be shared with others, who may build their vision of success based on a personal transmission of values and ideas. When a leader creates the culture and direction of a team with the purpose of hastening a vision, the journey to Mt. Olympus has already begun. Teams increase the chance that all members find their way to the top. The leader may end up building many other leaders in the process.

## SUCCESS BEHAVIOR #3: LIVING BY VALUES

The successful people in my sample told me that living by values is an essential leadership behavior. It is hard to judge people by values, because we each make different value choices. Even though we have different values, an individual may remain consistent with a set of principles, understandable to others. People come to depend on a leader who acts reliably; the person who is consistent with his or her values assures others that this person is dependable.

Success will reflect what one chooses. How one person builds a success will be as different for that person, just as individual values are different.

Leaders work in accord with their values; it should be easy for people around the leader to state what those values are. The actions of the leader make those values quite visible, as the leader works consistently in accord with a set of principles. When the leader must make hard decisions, one can understand the values as they are in practice, not simply what the leader says. When President Richard Nixon declared "I am not a crook," those were his words—but many people felt betrayed by his actions, which appeared crooked. When you work with people closely over time, you come to understand through their words and actions what they value.

Chris, an internet entrepreneur, told me that leaders demonstrate their values to employees and pass on their personal commitment to the work of the group.

> The biggest one here, for our company, is that you lead by example. We have a core set of values and we expect all of our employees to abide by those values and live them. If you see a leader who is not living by those, it's a really big deal. By ensuring client success, the leader's acts ensure you have integrity.

Leaders pass on values by leading by example. No other method has the impact as the consistent demonstration by the leader of what is really important. In addition, when the leader models performance behavior, the leader also shows followers that their work is valued.

Kirk, a business and software consultant with a Ph.D. in computer science, has operated his consulting practice for over 20 years.

> A lot of it is living a model life. If people can take a look at you and see that you live the life that you preach...to me it's just being honest. I really try to emphasize to the people that are under me—even though sometimes people don't want to hear the truth—that the truth can be told in a way that's uplifting, encouraging, and constructive. That's really what I try to do. I just want to pass on some of my skills to people who are following me.

Kirk and Chris both encourage other leaders to live the lives of their values, and to show people what those values look like in practice. Your life is a showcase for the critical values, and hopefully other people model the values as well as the success strategies of the leader. The leader not only demonstrates the values, but shows followers how to live in accord with those principles.

Chris added, "We have a value which is 'speed with purpose,' which is not just moving fast, but moving in a direction that is appropriate." I visited his organization, and observed that the employees applied focus and reached their goals with intense activity. The workplace appeared to be abuzz with intensity and definiteness of action. "Speed with purpose" teaches an employee how to make decisions.

Felix, a security consultant, practices a value that guides his personal behavior; his choice is to "live by your beliefs." He told me that all leaders should demonstrate their values by the way they live.

> Don't impose them on others and you will find amicable solutions to the resolution of a problem, understanding ethical dilemmas. Know that in the decision-making process, you have to consider ethical considerations in how you lead people. Know the standard, know yourself, know human nature, and understand your job.

Following his career in the U.S. Army, Felix now teaches workplace safety and the prevention of violence. For him, the work of a leader is to spread his or her values by the actions of business and life. Every decision creates an opportunity to demonstrate one's ethical priorities.

We all face dilemmas, but a leader may face ethical challenges more frequently than others, because all of the tension and choice tends to get directed to the person in charge. A leader who acts in accord with a consistent set of values tells others that "this is the way we work," without using a lot of words. Followers can see what this means. People understand the real priorities when they see how a leader makes decisions.

Leaders consistently apply their values and influence others to act with them—and these actions accelerate success. Imagine the focus created by a small group of people, all following the same vision, all working with similar values. As this group becomes experienced in working together, less time is needed to justify their actions; more time can be applied to direct business execution. The team applies synergistic action—all directed in the same ethical manner—toward a common purpose.

Living with values demonstrates high integrity; it colors one's character so that everyone can perceive the halo of truth that one has prepared. Working with values helps one to be successful by showing all present and future clients that this leader delivers with honor, trust, and goodness. As a team of people will choose to work under the same banner, those qualities of integrity, honesty, trust, and integrity are seen clearly by a greater number of people. Success comes with assurance and speed.

## SUCCESS BEHAVIOR #4: HELPING OTHER PEOPLE

If you are climbing Mt. Olympus, don't travel alone. Create your team to help you reach the summit. Help other people become successful, and they will help you achieve your success too. With a traveling team, you can lighten the load, accelerate the process of learning, and share moments of wit and humor.

*Helping other people* was one of the top leadership strategies mentioned by the people I interviewed. A number of people found ways to agree that leaders help others. Leadership is not just about giving commands; it is about helping people.

When leaders help people move forward, they do a number of positive things:

- Instruct others
- Inspire others
- Provide physical assistance
- Assure continuity
- Provide hope that changes will not defeat the people

Leadership is a social activity. It is not about silent reflection—although it may begin there. A person who fails to influence other people is not working as a leader. The best leaders develop the skills in other persons, often inspiring the development of leadership in others. Many successful people point to an influential mentor who showed the way forward or challenged them to do their best work. The experienced guide often recommends well-considered risk in order to build skills and competencies.

I think Jessica, a nonprofit leader and business owner, explains very well why helping other people helps the leader to become successful.

> I really struggled at that time to figure out, first, how do I make this work? And, second, how do I find work full time and do this? The answer I found was "no," I couldn't do both full time and volunteer, and so I cut back on the full-time employment to half-time. But then I realized that to make the nonprofit work, I had to build up leaders around me.

Leadership is an activity that leverages your time. Every successful person faces two big constraints: limited time and a limited budget. When a leader creates new leaders, more time is freed up. The process of helping other people does take an investment of time; this may seem daunting to folks feeling pressured by the work ahead of them. Jessica and other leaders have reported that helping people to do their work can have a time-bending quality to it: Your time has more impact because of the circle of colleagues, followers, and leaders around the enterprise.

Technology and IT CEO Simer told me that the best leaders don't just help people—they *serve* them.

> There is a concept called servant leadership. I'm learning that myself right now. I think leadership is about helping other people become better leaders. If you can do that, you will be very successful.

You may be like me. I was repelled by the concept of servant leadership when I first heard about it. I had images of a servant cleaning another person's foot—an image taken from the Bible. I have let the picture go now, and I believe that there is a spiritual dimension to our work as leaders. The servant leader is willing to make sure that he or she can help others. In the process one's own needs are satisfied. If the leader has a big enough purpose, he or she can adjust personal motivation to promote a better world. The leader joins others in walking into this future. As I see it, the servant leader's attention is on helping other people reach their goals.

Simer's company has grown by following this philosophy, and he has hundreds of people working to make technology work effectively for the rest of us. As I talked to him, I strongly sensed that his passion is genuine. Others have told me that he has carried this philosophy forward from a youth in India. Simer has wanted to help people improve their lifestyle and health.

Karen Malta describes herself as "the caring connector." She is an advocate for peace and a TV spokesperson; she also consults for a government agency which works in justice and law. "I create a win-win-win, or I'm not in," she told me several times. Karen also has a well-developed view of how leaders can help other people.

> I like to think of my role as more of a coach of the sports program. Everybody comes to that program with different backgrounds, skills, experiences, desires, and dreams. And the trick is to find some way to make them feel that they can accomplish what they want to accomplish in their life by getting them to experience what they are doing right here right now in the moment.

Karen treats people uniquely. She may have a desire to reach a goal with her program, but she takes the time to discover how the people around her are different. She believes in coaching people to success, rather than ordering people to submit to her direction.

Coaching will involve building a guiding relationship, which includes knowledge and appreciation, challenge, and support. Many people work with a coach to provide accountability. The coach can follow the progress of the individual, noting progress and challenging the person to go further. Accountability means that the coach is expecting deliverable results on schedule and asking the learner to become stronger in their actions and more determined in their efforts. Without doubt, an accountability coach helps most learners achieve more goals than they would by themselves. An excellent coach can help a person select goals that are highly meaningful and can be sustained over time.

I've described leadership as a social process. People follow leaders because they like them, but also because they believe in the rightness of their work. Social connection is an active factor that changes how people work. Leaders not only help people move ahead, they amend the direction of the other person's movement. Once initiated, followers tend to keep working in the same direction—call it positive dynamic inertia. When the leader leads with service and coaches for excellence, people tend to achieve a lot. This power to build other people serves the leader's success as well. Imagine having the power of dynamic inertia working to support your success.

## SUCCESS BEHAVIOR #5: BE PERSISTENT

Is this the most common success factor ever flogged by motivational speakers—perhaps to the point of being cliché? Nevertheless, my interviewees told me repeatedly, "If you want to be successful, don't quit." The most famous Calvin Coolidge quotation tells us why the persistence factor is essential to our efforts.

> Nothing in the world can take the place of persistence. Talent will not; nothing is more common than unsuccessful men with talent. Genius will not; unrewarded genius is almost a proverb. Education will not; the world is full of educated derelicts. Persistence and determination alone are omnipotent.

That might be the most famous remembered detail about the 30th president, who was known for doing little except for presiding over an era described at the time as "The Coolidge Prosperity."

I heard the word persistence in different ways from my interview subjects. I began by labeling this quality as "don't quit." Leaders and successful people keep going. Their vision drives them forward. They believe that they will achieve something great. Until they get there, the leader will focus on continuing to apply efforts, pushing forward, and learning through the process. An emerging successful person has already made the decision to try again, although the method for driving forward may change.

The persistent person has a destination in mind and continues daily to reach that place. In order to make progress, the leader will continue with the strategy until it no longer seems to create value. Then the leader will try another tactical method to reach that goal. Persistence may involve changing the methods, but the vision of success should not change, at least not often.

Bob, an attorney, seminar leader, and head of an international non-profit, faced the challenge of continuing his business after walking away from a plane crash.

> What I've learned through all the leadership, no matter what the obstacle or challenge, or how bad it seems, you can't quit. I still had to put food on the table, I still had bills to pay, and I figured out what to do, I did what I had to do, and I'm still in business today. A month after I opened my sole proprietorship, I was in a plane crash.

He reported good health, no physical damage—yet imagine the impact on his psyche after surviving a crash. It would be as though a mighty Olympian god had hurled him to the earth, saying, "I don't care what your plans are. You are going where I say you go." Anyone would feel humbled, yet Bob built a vital business and served as an inspirational leader to tens of thousands of people.

Patti, a marketing guru, spoke passionately about the power of persistence.

> The number-one lesson in my leadership training is to be consistent. You can't say enough on that really. You can go over it and over it, but until people really see, because of the society we live in today, they're real quick to give up.

Patti built her business promoting the boogie board, first in California, later around the world. When she started, the boogie board was a concept originated by her friends in the early 1970s as an alternative to the surfboard. Patti built her business by driving to surf shops along the West Coast, demonstrating its use. She described herself as a "surfer chick," working out of the back of her car, knocking on doors and building interest one person at a time. Eventually, the market reached a tipping point, and the boogie board became a massive hit with surfers. In a few years, a larger enterprise with worldwide distribution channels bought the business. Like many other recreational products, Patti worked hard as a personal envoy to build a market until the crowd demanded more product than a small business could provide. Persistence and consistency made this happen.

Commitment leads a person to become persistent and successful. Ryan, a wealth management expert and sales manager who leads a team of financial advisors, is responsible for recruiting, training, and motivating his sales force as he has grown in his role over the last 13 years. "The commitment level is showing everybody that you are still committed," he said. Commitment and staying in the game are necessary, because your emotions—which go up and down—are an unreliable force for moving forward. When the leader doesn't feel like doing the work, but does so regardless, it strengthens the behavioral actions that lead to success. The committed person pushes forward, and this creates a successful habit.

What is success? Suga, a peace activist, poet, and teacher, told me plainly that he creates his success through his persistence.

> I would say success is the fuel to push pass the obstacles so that I can achieve what I want to achieve. Because if I didn't possess certain leadership skills and qualities when certain obstacles and other stumbling blocks came up, I would retreat. I would go back and give up and try something different. My faith in myself, my belief, my passion, my love for what I do, and my dreams are what keep me going. That's success.

Push past the obstacles and have faith. Suga teaches us that we have some innate skills to create the power and energy to move past the roadblocks. When we keep up our effort, we strengthen our natural talent, and people tell us "you are a leader." We reinforce these skills through our regular, daily efforts. They don't seem remarkable at all. But when built up over time—and our big purpose and faith in our self can help us keep going—the behavior seems nearly heroic to others, and we can get classed as a leader. Our success habits can start small, but they become huge when repeatedly practiced. As Suga advises us, "Have love for what you do." Know your dreams and be persistent.

Clark, the CEO of a telecommunications firm, talked to me about leadership and persistence. To him, being persistent is part of the process of growth. In our interview, Clark reminded me how many of the great people in history achieved incredible success only after they persisted past the point where most would have given up. Persistence is a quality that helps to make us appear immortal and legendary in the memories of others. Successful people have taken their vision beyond the point where reasonable people would have given up.

To all of you who would be successful: Think about your vision for a better future and keep thinking about it. Do something every day that helps your vision become part of our reality. Build a habit that takes you further than the average person around you. Your vision is worth it!

## SUCCESS BEHAVIOR #6: BE A LEADER WITH A VISION

Without a vision, a leader is more like a manager—interested in preserving the status quo, or in achieving modest goals. Some people change the game, point the team around them toward a lofty destination, and inspire action. No one is inspired by goals that are raised by 2%; this is dull, this is not leadership, and this is not the sigil of success. A vision redefines the way people work and shows everyone that what they are doing today is simply the platform leading up to a better world.

A vision may start as a spark, an uncertain idea. It can grow into a clearer picture as the leader cherishes the vision. Think of cultivating a beautiful image, such as watering a young tree in the garden. The fledgling tree may need help getting started. After the vision builds its roots, it finds strength of its own. The leader is like a caring gardener who nourishes the vision, and shares it regularly with people who are receptive to this new idea.

Does the leader "own" the vision? Visions can have a life of their own and can be shared as a transmission of vital data between kindred souls. With the leader's help, these bold ideas may rock the world.

People with vision often can "see" the future; they develop a clear image that can be described by others. One way to build a vision is to imagine what it looks like and to return frequently to this picture. I like to add details to my vision as I return to it; I find ways to paint the vision of the world by doing things that support the vision's emergence. With practice, the vision becomes clearer and brighter, and I believe it becomes easier to share the possibility held in the vision with others.

Paul, a serial entrepreneur, has moved through a number of business ventures. When he ended one business partnership, he had no solid plans for his future, only a vision.

> I turned to my wife and I said, "That chapter has closed. What else can we wind up doing?" I wound up building a beautiful spec house. I made more money on that spec house than I had made in the previous five years or more in my business.

Paul was surprised how fruitful this vision was, and how quickly he created a new way of working for himself by building a number of high-quality properties. He shortly found that his way of working attracted new clients to his new company, and he was kept busy building residences and commercial properties for a number of years. His wife is also a business professional and sales champion; Paul ended up building a new business location for her company offices. Paul's wife became president of a specialty motor vehicle company with a superb reputation. With enthusiasm, Paul told me how important it was for him to share and cultivate his business vision with his wife. This couple has supported each other for decades, helping each other to be successful even as the character of their activities changed dramatically.

Having a vision is useful for guiding a team on creative and commercial products. Patrick, an applications game leader for a major U.S. corporation, spoke to me about why vision is important in designing games for handheld devices. He leads a team of applications designers who bring their games to the marketplace.

> On the execution side, strong vision and focus are important. If people do not know what the idea is, or if everyone on the project does not know what we are trying to accomplish, they are not going to be able to help us.

> Let's say you have 10 employees working on a project. If you are not trying to define what they are doing, if you don't lay out A/B/C/D for every single employee, you will have one employee going off in one direction, another going off this way; you want everyone efficiently working toward one goal.

> The most important consideration is focus. Vision. Communicating that vision. At any great company, doing something that's great, you will find a leader who is a very good speaker, a communicator and what she says is, "What we are doing here is this. It's awesome, it's special." When everyone agrees, they will sprint toward that thing she is saying.

People are energized by a vivid vision—especially when a leader steps forward and points, "This way!" Patrick believes and works with this philosophy; he does not want to bury his employees with details. His hope is to inspire action that takes the project forward. He focuses his project on a single goal and encourages individual and effort—hard work that takes the project forward, but with passion. Raises or bonuses alone cannot inspire this kind of passionate action. People work hard on a goal because they see and understand the vision, and they feel the sincerity of the leader.

Michelle had a vision that led her away from her career as a physician in private practice. She wanted to help people create success for themselves by making healthy food choices and living consciously. By providing the knowledge and methods of living with greater health, she made a career transition that took her away from being a traditional doctor providing individual consultations. She started by leading small groups with patients on living with optimal health. She realized that the best way she could make an impact on the largest number of people was through speaking, writing, and leading seminars to the general public.

Michelle told me what lies at the heart of her vision:

> I really have a heart for people who struggle with food. Because that's where my personal passion comes from—I discovered my own struggle with that. In order to be able to help others, I had to be able to be successful at running a business and influencing and inspiring people.

Vision led to a change in the way Michelle works. She told me that it became necessary to have "the ability to clarify a vision, to see something in a bigger way, and to see what's possible." As Michelle proceeded to work on her idea, she was then able to put the team into processes, and apply the tactics and strategies into place to make that vision come true. Eventually, Michelle found that her new work allowed her to influence the field of eating on a scale that was never possible for her before.

I think that Michelle has been able to move effectively in this work because her vision and her passion have been in alignment. The more that she applied herself to this new way of working, the more that she enjoyed the results she created. Michelle told me,

> I do not know how this sounds, but I feel that I have a moral obligation to effectively share this message, because I know this changes lives. It's changed mine. I've seen the effect that it has on people. If I allow my limitations or my fear to limit my resources in any way, then we're not going to be

able to help other people. That would be nothing short of a shame!

Not only did Michelle feel the joy of working in this area, she has adopted a moral obligation to do this job. Her success includes helping other people, reaching goals and becoming more productive in the way she works. As she has worked, moving forward her dreams, she has discovered a new form of motivation for pushing forward: she wants—needs!—to help other people live healthy lives. There is a discovered drive for entrepreneurs, knowing that they can help other people; they may discover it will be *wrong not to do so.*

Vision pushes us profoundly, once we identify with it. If you connect with an idea, you may have to become its servant. The pull of action may be profound. You may be the spokesperson for the vision, but you won't own it by yourself—others near you may share a connection with this big idea, and it may change their lives as well. Be grateful that you are not on this journey alone.

## FINAL THOUGHTS: BECOMING SUCCESSFUL THROUGH LEADERSHIP ACTION

I like to think that leadership helps people derive more value out of their life, both for the leaders and followers. I also believe that successful people create a success through a contribution to a better world. We can find exceptions to both of these statements, I know, but I believe in the virtue of servant leadership and success that has helped others.

Leaders do many different things. In my interview group, I was told that these leadership behaviors create success:

- Believing in your decisions, having confidence
- Creating a team
- Living by values
- Helping other people
- Being consistent/persistent
- Working from a vision

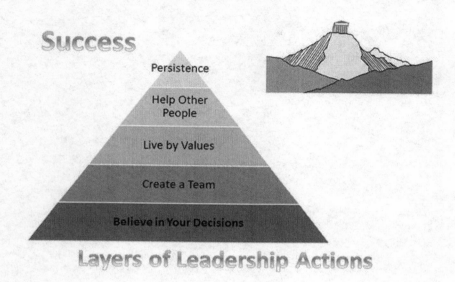

## DR. STEVE'S TIP

Choosing to be a leader may help you become successful. If you do this right, you may also change the lives of many people for the better, which will leave you feeling fulfilled. You may earn your financial success by helping other people create their rainbows.

Develop other leaders, and the people near you will help you climb Mt. Olympus. Demonstrate genuine caring for others, and share your values. Help people grow into their leadership skills; for most of us, we have to learn our leadership lessons the hard way. Until we grow into the role, many of us suffer a significant amount of resistance from those who instinctively dislike authority—even someone who has their best interests at heart!

To get them on your side, show them first that you will help them climb the mountain. Offer both advice and muscle. Help others to be independent. Be persistent. You know that you will face setbacks. Show others that your vision is big enough to take you beyond the next hill. Start each day expecting to win.

# Chapter 7: Leaders Stumble…and That's Not All

*Fall down seven times.*
*Stand up eight times.*
*~ Japanese proverb*
*I remember falling on a night time hike. I didn't see the ground in front of me; I was descending rapidly over rocks. All of a sudden, I wasn't on solid ground. My foot had turned, and began falling,* slowly it seemed, but I couldn't stop. My head hit the rocks below me. Even though the impact wasn't hard, I felt the \*BANG\* as my forehead made contact with rocks. My arms were out in front of me, and I got scratched up protecting my fall. I picked myself up with the help of friends, and realized that my fall could have been much worse.*

*I've stumbled while hiking as well as in my professional life. You likely have your own steep journey ahead of you. Your journey up to the summit, your Mt. Olympus, will likely involve those experiences of falling, just as I did. The journey to achieve something meaningful will include moments of steep ascent, and a winding path. Stumbling is part of the leader's journey.*

*Leaders don't stop after they stumble. They assess their situation and gather their energy. They call for help. The main point is that they keep going. Mt. Olympus is mighty, however all successful people have faced their own private challenge. It is what happens after the stumble that counts.*

I've learned one profound truth from interviewing successful people: Everyone stumbles. The path to success involves getting knocked down, and still continuing after that point. A stumble is that point of difficulty where you must face a challenge that shouldn't have happened, or that you didn't want or expect. Nevertheless, it must be dealt with.

I prefer using the word stumble to the "F" word—failure—because the latter suggests a judgment, personal limitations, or a sense of defeat. Stay in a failure condition too long, and it begins to define the next steps.

When you have moved beyond a tremendous challenge and look back, you can usually say, "Parts of that were difficult. I had doubts. The good thing is that I didn't stay there. I am now moving forward again." By persisting beyond a challenge, you earn the right to call it a stumble.

Motivational speaker W. Mitchell has stumbled. Burned over large parts of his body, and then surviving a plane crash that left him paralyzed, he assessed his choices. "Before I was paralyzed, there were 10,000 things I could do," he said. "Now there are 9,000. I can either dwell on the 1,000 I've lost, or I can focus on the 9,000 I have left." Having heard him speak, I have been impressed with the power and spirit this man, this decision. Will you be focused on the limitations of your situation? The truth is that you still have powerful choices ahead of you, and the opportunity to create your next success.

There are moments in everyone's life that are challenging. What happens after a fall is a defining moment and often the source for lasting stories. Leaders don't stay down. Successful people know that there is a path forward, and the road forward depends on your actions and attitudes.

Barbara Fredrickson's book, *Positivity* (2009), influenced my life and what I talk about in everyday business. She demonstrates through evidence and examples that a positive mind can change the way you work in the world. (Part of my journey in creating this book was enjoying the narrative of many successful people as they told me how they moved forward past the point of stumbling. I looked for some of that magic elixir for myself.)

The joy of presenting this book, and especially this chapter, is that I can now share some of the powerful ideas that I have heard about moving past the stumbles. Here is what leaders do to create their success.

## DON'T QUIT

Stuff happens. Don't stop moving forward. Be consistent, and be persistent. Keep playing the game. Every day is a new opportunity to win, roll the dice again. Successful people stay in the game, keep taking the initiative, and putting their work on the line.

Sharon Lechter is the author of many books that have changed people's lives, including *Think and Grow Rich – Three Feet from Gold* and *Outwitting the Devil,* written with the cooperation of the Napoleon Hill Foundation. She shared her thoughts on success and stumbling with me.

> I think we all stumble. Napoleon Hill said it best: "Every adversity, every barrier, generates the seed of an equivalent or greater benefit." This happens to me, and I'm sure it happens to your readers as well, you have a mind about how something is going to go. You've envisioned what's going to happen, and then it doesn't happen that way. You create your own frustration, your own stress, because you have this vision of how it should've happened—instead of trusting that it will work out the way it should have.
>
> We've all had setbacks, and certainly I've had business dealings that I was sure we were going to consummate, get done, and then something happens. The door closes, and I get really frustrated. But then I stop myself. When one door closes, another one opens. And so it's that the leadership skill of persistence, of having the end in mind, and of knowing that if one path doesn't work out the way you expected, another one will.

Leaders move forward, and sometimes they barely notice the disruption to their progress. Deborah was executive vice president of one of the largest private banks in her state; her portfolio was titled "wealth management." Today, she has transcended her work in banking and is looking to define her work on her terms, in new ways. Deborah's work is expanding in her encore career. Her direction is still unfolding and defining itself; her work will include a book about leadership, the nature of the brain, and women, and taking women on transformational discovery tours to places like Nepal and Bali. Deborah told me,

> I think by quickly identifying what the opportunities are, where I wanted to go, putting a plan behind it, and then working to execute on that plan—there was never time to stumble. I was too busy. If I stumbled, I jumped right back up and dusted myself off and was on my way again.

Deborah's direction has always been forward. She doesn't dwell on the disruption of the moment; she is working to reach her next goal. Because she has always been in motion, and her focus is forward, she barely notices those experiences that I have called a stumble and that others might call a failure. She has a habit of simply moving forward, consistently.

In the martial arts, there is a common story told about the founder of Aikido, a man named Morihei Ueshiba. One day, a student remarked, "Sensei, you never seem to make a mistake!" He then corrected his student: "Oh, I make mistakes all the time. But you don't see them, because I have learned to correct my mistakes faster than most people can notice." That is an advantage of mastery and lifelong training—we correct our mistakes faster than most people. We may seem to be flawless, and we really aren't. The successful person keeps on pressing toward the goal, and the corrections come faster than most people believe is possible. Deborah exhibits this "fast correct" quality when she stumbles.

Do you get distracted by competing calls to your attention? When I spoke to Stephen, a speaker, author, philanthropist, and corporate trainer on corporate wellness, I heard him speak of many issues that are similar in my life. I asked him, "Do you ever stumble?"

> I face that challenge every day. I've become very aware of procrastination and rejection. There are always elements of procrastination and rejection—they don't go away. They always present themselves at the next level of what you are working on, because there is always an element of "Well, I guess I will take a little time off today, because I think I've done enough." In actual fact, you may just need to push through that procrastination piece. And the rejection piece is always that little niggling thing that sits on your shoulder and wants to go, "No one is going to read that. No one wants to hear that." I've got to brush that off my shoulder and keep going. Those things are always there.

Are you kept from making progress because of procrastination and rejection? Highly effective people don't delay when they know what has to be done, yet you find yourself opening Facebook for just three minutes or watching silly videos. Once you are distracted, it takes a lot of energy and determination to get back on track. At every moment, you may need to make a choice, "Go back to my biggest purpose? Or look at cute animal pictures?"

Do you slow down due to feelings of rejection? Stephen spoke about feelings of rejection that slowed down the speed of his project completion—an internal voice that tells him that "no one will be interested." We all have a similar voice of judgment in our heads, but if what you are doing is valuable and is going to change the world for the better, you can't let it slow your progress.

Sharon Lechter, who is also a CPA and advocate for financial literacy, told me,

> In my business, which is financial education, I've been working with schools, governments, politicians, and consumers. Each one of those avenues has lots of disappointments. Lots of red tape. Lots of frustration. You can stop at the first sign of a "no" or you can say, "OK, that's not going to work. What's next?" When you have your vision, and for me, my vision is financial education, I only say, "I'm not going to waste any more time with this individual, or on this path. Let's find another way."
>
> And so it's that persistent, never-give-up attitude that a leader has to have in order to continue inspiring their team.

Leaders and successful people will face barriers. Sharon mentioned government red tape and the frustration that comes with it. I know from the vantage point of a small business owner that I have had a wonderful plan—for a child care center, for a charter school, or for a new place to work—and I have faced restrictions that are written into the law that challenge a person to stop, avoid anything innovative, any new ideas, and to proceed with the same old, same old formula.

The person with the persistent mind finds a way to move forward. A stop sign in the path simply means that there is more work to come. Intelligence applied to problems in the spirit of positivity often can provide an alternate route. Success is achieved through pushing forward and regularly achieving goals.

## TIME TO IMPROVE YOURSELF

My friend Dan describes himself as a seminar junkie. He likes to attend workshops and transformational seminars. Changing his life for the better is something that he is interested in—he is always paying attention to life's lessons, both from his own experiences, and from those of others. I have learned that many people enjoy the process of continual self improvement. Other people don't have time for it, and they would rather not sit in classes and seminars.

Are you a learner? Do you work to improve yourself? Can you describe what you would like to learn in the next two years?

The successful people I interviewed have a strong interest in improving themselves. When they stumble or face a setback, a popular strategy is to find ways to improve themselves. Leaders get better at doing many things, *including* getting better at the things they are already good at doing.

Want to win a horse race? You have to be strong and disciplined. Do you want to win races against other winners? You have to get *even better* at the things you are already doing well. The winner of the high-stakes horse race may take first by a nose. To succeed against other successful people, you must be at least marginally better in some way—because depending on good luck isn't a strategy. Successful people and leaders decide to improve themselves.

Elaine, an entrepreneur who created an advertising agency, believes in her people, wants to help her clients become successful, and builds advertising success through hard analytics—even when using traditional print advertising channels. She told me,

> I'm a leader. Which means I have to be good. That's my job. I have to be good at doing leadership things. Like running good meetings; like inspiring people; like motivating people; or painting vision pictures; helping people see the direction that we're going; helping people decide if they want to be part of that direction; helping them move on if they don't.

Elaine's product is advertising; nevertheless, she sees herself in the people-building business. She understands the idea that building her skills as a leader is essential toward her commercial success.

Bill is an engineer who launched a successful software business more than 30 years ago. He says,

> If you're not making mistakes, you're not doing anything. You have to keep learning from them unless you want to keep making the same mistakes over and over again.

And turning his attention to moments when he has stumbled,

> I would have to say more than just leadership skills per se; it has been real self-examination. Other people give me their

impressions of what they see in me during those difficult times. I just refocus, work hard, and that's how I've recovered from it.

In addition to hard work, Bill chooses to learn about himself. He pays attention to what other people have told him. His moments of stumbling are natural outcomes of taking action. He is a humble man who has learned a lot about the skill of public speaking and continues to enter contests and refine his skill in speaking and influence. Moreover, Bill has had results, working with grace and good will.

John is a successful physician who has pioneered new applications of technology to remove tumors, often cancerous, using a cybernetic tool. He has worked around highly intelligent people his entire professional career in medical teams that are small businesses, and he confessed to me that "No one trained me to be a business leader in medical school." Instead, he had to learn his organizational skills while he was doing it, and often without the advantage of a good mentor. In his words,

> There are always different challenges, different setbacks. Unless you are in solo practice, at least for a physician or even for anyone if you are in a solo business, you don't have a lot of personal dynamics. But for me I've always been in groups. A group has different personal and professional issues; the group that I'm in now was very large. We had some challenges with our leadership...the group basically dissolved.
>
> Different partners went in different directions; they formed their own groups and did different things. That was a big challenge. It was the stumbling in the effect of a single large successful group fragmented into smaller groups. We were dysfunctional for a while; for me personally and my group, all of those activities that had to be done to have a successful group were now falling on us individually, where previously they had been done by other members of the group.
>
> So the idea of reaching out and finding resources to get that information, to get that experience, get those skills and find people to help you do that, is kind of a basic activity that leaders must have.

## HELPING OTHERS

Successful people help other people out, and for them, this is a leadership behavior. I did not expect to find this response with the strength and repetition that I did, as far as its ability to get beyond one's stumbling.

Think about it this way: When you help others, you must turn your attention away from your own situation, and apply real efforts for another.

Could it be that too much self-focus is detrimental? A person on the road to success has already worked on tactics that will take him or her forward. From what I have heard from my interviews, my success informants, we must be willing to push others forward as well as ourselves. A person with too much self-focus simply reaches diminishing returns.

Dave, a master sales professional, author and executive coach, told me that just looking out for yourself won't help a person reach success. His business includes a non-profit service.

> The most important lesson that I want to teach people is the power of collaboration, and the power of teamwork. I remember when I was teaching soccer for a group of 12-year-old kids. My son looked at the roster and the team and my son said to me "Dad there's going to be a problem." "Why?" "Because Bobbie and Johnny don't get along." "What you mean they don't get along?" "They fight in school all the time." I said, "They're on the same team they're going to figure it out."

> So on the very first day of practice, sure enough, Bobbie comes up and goes "Johnny's on this team! I hate Johnny!" And I said "Time out. He's your teammate. I don't care what you do outside of this but on your team he's your guy. You guys are going to take care of each other and protect each other because you're on the same team. So don't talk like that." In the end, whenever they fought before that, it didn't matter. It was last time they fought.

> That's the lesson I want to teach people. You can't be successful by yourself. If you believe you can – you can walk on people's backs and get to some outcome. At the end of the day, if you haven't made a difference, you might have made yourself happy, but you haven't made a difference.

And, how you keep score in the world or how the world keep score on you, whatever is – is are you making a difference in the lives of others.

Leaders are able to climb Mt. Olympus, in part, because they have other people who work with them. How do leaders inspire incredible commitment and devotion? At least part of the answer, I believe, is that leaders make investments in other people. Leaders serve others, in fact, by offering their talents, their time, their experience, and their emotional support.

A sane reaction to stumbling, then, is to take the focus off of your own situation, and to decide, "I will help others." As in the song "Turn! Turn! Turn!" sung by the Byrds and adapted from the Book of Ecclesiastes, "to everything there is a season, and a time to every purpose under heaven." After stumbling, it may simply not be the right time to push forward energetically, but it may now be a rational time to help others with their purposes. As all things turn, at a later date (and perhaps not too distant) the leader will again be able make strong progress toward his victory. That leader will have new alliances and friendship working with him. Success becomes easier when one can go with the flow, and realize that progress must come in another area: helping others.

I heard this idea from the words of my interview responders. Jessica created a business and a non-profit organization shortly after she and her husband were simultaneously let go from their corporate jobs. She decided that she had a big purpose ahead of her: helping professional people find work after career upheaval, just as she had. Jessica told me,

> I stumbled because I didn't yet understand how important it is to help others. I was doing everything on my own and delegating or saying, "I need this done." What I needed to do was to have a group of core leaders around me that would take the big chunks and delegate them, and work with their volunteers and invest in their volunteers.
>
> That was the stumbling part of getting that working. I have a core team of five now, and a board of directors of eight that have stepped up to those roles. I pour into them. I invest my time with and then they invest all their time with so everybody else is under their umbrella.

This leader felt overwhelmed by the challenges facing her. For Jessica, the most rational course was to build other leaders near her. She was building a business as well as a non-profit organization, and she needed everyone to do their part in a big way. Challenging people to be leaders in their work, even as she offered her help for their growth, seemed to be the best way to create the leadership talent that Jessica needed to move forward.

One of my respondents told me how important it was to help others do their jobs their way—as long as it did not interfere with the organizational purpose. Ed has been a successful speaker and author; he has also been a college professor and leader of several non-profit organizations. He told me that when he was brought in as head of a professional association as its executive director, he started making decisions about placing people in offices—completely ignoring the previous arrangements and the ways people had already learned to work. This was Ed's big stumble:

> The point I'm getting to is that we had just hired a new meeting manager, and one of our people asked me, "Ed, where you going to put Dawn?" "Well, I'm going to give her Caroline's office." Well, I detected a little bit of reluctance—a little something—there were some nonverbal messages going on. I went to one woman and said, "You've been here a long time. If you want, you're welcome to take Caroline's office." She said, "Oh, no, no, no, I'm very happy where I am."
>
> So I went to three other people, who were also senior in the service, and all three of them to a person said that they didn't want to make this change; they were very happy in their cubicles.

Ed discovered that even though he was *the boss,* he was stepping into a new culture, and he could defy the existing ways (including where people had their space) *or* he could learn how to get the best results with people. He chose to follow his instincts and learn more about the culture of the workplace—this was the best course to get results with the people who work there. Ed also told this story to emphasize *how important* the relations are with the people who work for him:

Another point I learned a long time ago, at the university, was when one of the staff people came to my office, and said, "Ed, do you have a minute?" "Oh, of course. Sure, Jerry." And I'm shuffling papers and doing this and that. He stood there for a minute and a half, and then said, "I will come back later."

A few minutes later, the phone rings, and it was him. He called me on the phone. And what I learned there was that if I had just set the papers aside, let the phone ring, and have eye-to-eye contact with him, I would have shown Jerry respect. It's a small thing! Trivial at the time, trivial. It was a good learning point about recognizing and respecting other people.

Ed learned that in order to be an effective leader, he had to keep his awareness open to the people who worked with him. He wants to help people—many of us are like that—yet we are so caught up in our own world of distraction and challenges that we sometimes live in a trance world. It is easy just to think of our own needs. Ed realized that helping others was important for his journey forward, and that to be effective, he needed to keep a mindful attitude toward the calls for help he heard.

The phase of work that I call the stumble is certainly a challenging one. A natural reaction of all of us is to turn inward, mend our own hurt and pain—but it can be a valuable time to help others as well. Perhaps our work helping others is a bold signal of our positive nature; others assess us and our sincere effort to do good by others. By doing so, the leader may create lasting allegiance to their own ventures—creating long-term gains in exchange for sincere moments of service.

## LEARNING FROM STUMBLES

I ask people regularly, "What do you need to learn in order to be highly successful?" I am surprised at how often people have no definite idea in mind of what should be learned, yet people generally know they need to keep learning. The person who stumbles in his journey forward gets the chance to learn something. The most successful people have learned a lot—and sometimes it is painful! The moment of stumbling is like the world smacking you on the side of the head: "Hey, watch where you're going!"

In creating new successes—whether in relationships, careers, financial, health, or sports—learning is essential. We simply don't know what we don't know. We may know that other people have created success similar to what we want to build, or that Mt. Olympus can be climbed and conquered. But like the hiker gazing up the mountain, anticipating the route ahead, we cannot see all the twists and turns in the trail, or judge when we need to leave the path to get to the peak. We know that we must keep learning, and that if our goal is worthy and significant, we will be transformed by the time we reach the top.

Learning is necessary to make a worthy ascent. Stumbling tells us that we may need to expand our curriculum. Leading the way up Mt. Olympus is going to change the way we work. Becoming aware of this can be extremely valuable to a success seeker and leader.

It is hard to know where our own knowledge ends, or what it is possible to learn. Business builders always have more to learn about the nature of business, legal contracts, and government regulation. Managers and leaders continually need to refresh and expand what they practice in getting results with other people. Anyone working with technology will find it valuable to stay current with the world of software, applications, security, and collecting key performance indicators. These are only some of the many necessary areas of knowledge for a business leader—keeping in mind that success may come in an area unrelated to business, so there will always be vast learning available to us.

Learning is local. Much of what can be learned depends on "how it works here." In physics, we learn absolute truths that never change. In creating human systems and business enterprise, leaders learn that much of what is important to their work depends on what is around them. Context counts, and learning involves applying knowledge to different situations. Truth frequently changes when a leader works in the real world.

Learning gives you an advantage in moving forward after a stumble. Elaine, the advertising firm owner, told me,

> I have stumbled and I have had to pay the price. In the long run, I think this is learning, so stumbling is never a bad thing—you always learn something, it's just whether you are going to repeat that mistake or not.

People who have opened a business or started something new in any line of work have had to put their leadership to the test. The real world demands that systems fill a need, help people with their problems, or enhance the lives of others. In the process of launching the new project, reasonable people expect to face failure *somewhere.* The successes that come will enrich our lives; the moments of stumbling leave us with knowledge and learning, too. Successful people embrace the learning whenever their plans are thwarted. Entrepreneurs have built a vast internal library of learning applied to their line of work.

Dan built his business as a business coach after starting more than eight successful businesses and working more than 40 years in business and sales. Now he coaches privately with business owners to help them reach new levels of success. Dan told me that he has learned a lot from his experience:

> I had a client that asked me, "Why should I hire you?"
>
> I said, "I could probably give you a lot of reasons. The main reason is of all the needs that you have, I have probably faced them 20 times, and handled them wrong 10 of those times. I can not only help you get there successfully, I can help you avoid making the mistakes."
>
> He said, "You're hired!"

Dan then confirmed for me that the stumble is an accelerator on the route to success.

> Absolutely, I'm proud of some of my mistakes. They got me that much closer to success, faster.

Our knowledge and accumulated learning is a special kind of wealth. It allows us to transform our lives and fulfill our dreams. Stumbling shows us what we need to learn, and gives us the chance to set new priorities in the way we work.

One of my interview respondents sold his business and became a venture capitalist, serving on several company advisory boards in the process. Chris told me,

> Yes. I think we stumble all the time. I stumbled last night playing tennis. I'm still paying for it this morning!
>
> I think it's that old adage: It's not how you stumble, it's how quickly you get back up and move on, and learn from it. I think a lot of times what happens is you see people that fixate on an issue—they see it and can't get past it.

What's important is that you experience good and bad, and that from there, you have to treat them the same and you have to learn from them equally. You can't dwell on them; you just have to think on them, and then move past.

Chris confirms that the leader should learn from the stumble and get back into the game quickly. You can't maintain attention on issues that have already become history while anticipating what is coming up. The leader should learn to turn attention forward.

When learning from the past experience, Chris tells us that we should remember to treat both the good and bad experiences as sources of knowledge. He encourages emerging leaders to understand and move on—our attention should not keep going to the past.

Our actions today are under our control. No power on Earth allows us to change the past. We can choose to learn from recent events; and if the stumble hurts enough, we probably will be thinking about what is really important. The future is not entirely under our control, but with a prepared mind, a positive heart, and allies, an emerging leader can make choices today that increase the chances for success in the future. Learning from stumbles and failures teaches us what we need to know, and what is important.

## CHANGE YOUR PERCEPTION AND JUDGMENT OF FAILURE

As discussed at the outset of this chapter, I've chosen to describe challenges on the road to success as stumbles rather than failures, and I believe that's important because our words shape our thinking and attitudes. A judgment of "failure" suggests an indelible stamp on your character. The choice (this is a choice, folks!) to assign failure to one's work is a major limitation over future actions.

Look at what's happened again, and continue moving forward. It's not a failure if you can still move ahead and make progress. Never call yourself a failure—your sense of self-confidence and optimism are too important for your journey.

Your mind actively constructs the meaning of your actions. If you look at the facts, they will appear without judgment. Assigning a meaning is like telling a story about your own actions. If you think what happened to you is a failure, then that is how your mind will consider what you have done, and what you will do in the future.

In contrast, we all have choices to look at recent events and determine for ourselves, "I can learn from this. I know how to get better results in the future."

When challenges arrive, you need look at them with a fresh perspective. Instead of thinking, "I'm not good enough to solve that one!" reflect on how you will learn from what you went through. Understand that you can decide to learn and become stronger as you act near uncertainty.

Karen is a spiritual teacher and author; she specializes in "helping people have a joyous, peaceful, collaborative, stress-free, and orderly relationship with money." When we spoke about stumbling, Karen told me,

> My biggest stumbles have been early in my life: addiction, and a deep, deep surrender into a spiritual abyss. The leadership that I got out of all that was the capacity to understand human powerlessness in a positive way. I've learned to understand the extent to which my being smart and hardworking can get you really far, and then there is a place of grace that comes out of that. Being willing to surrender to a power greater than myself, to live a life that includes a higher power, that's really been essential to me as a leader.

It's OK to think of yourself as human, fallible, and capable of learning. You can be a leader to inspire others and do great things. Your attitude and mental resiliency is important when you stumble.

James, an author and entrepreneur, told me,

> One thing I have tried to learn how to do also is state the obvious. Babe Ruth probably said it the best, "Keep on going and the chances are you will stumble on something, perhaps when you are least expecting it." So, if you are one of those people who fixate on the negative, then it is going to limit your capacity and it doesn't make sense. It's like a mental habit. I think there is a lot to be learned from people who have been very effective in overcoming a significant failure. They categorize it in a way that is useful. That's all there is to it—not to dwell on it.

We are reminded that as we move to doing our important work, we increase the chances that we are going to stumble. If we want to avoid the stumble, we literally have to *stand still*—which is not a success strategy! Our choice as leaders and people dedicated to improving the world is to go forth, and stumbling will happen to us. We don't have to be fixated on the negative aspect of the stumble; we can learn how to move forward toward more positive outcomes.

Make your stumbles useful. You may have to get something fixed, you may have to wrap a wound, and you may need to build relationships. While you are recovering from a stumble, you will have the advantage of vulnerability—a useful state to show other people that you are real and fallible. The vulnerable leader demonstrates clearly to others, "I am dedicated to this vision; I am going to make this happen. Will you come with me?"

Business coach Dan confirmed for me that successful people have adopted a special attitude toward stumbling.

> It's true. One of the many ways that very successful people think differently from people who aren't as successful, is that they don't see failure as abject failure. It's really back to the old idea that for every failure that happens, you are one step closer to achieving it. It's a mentality.

Dan reminded me of the Edison's experimentation with materials, in trying to build a practical light bulb. An observer might say that testing a process over a thousand times is useless, evidence of being stuck.

> How else could you have the diligence, the drive, and the discipline to try an experiment 1,300 times? When asked how it felt to fail that many times, Edison said, "I didn't fail that many times, I found that many ways that didn't work."

Testing over and over is not a failure to a dedicated leader; it is persistence and learning. Successful people shift their thinking and mental attitude from failure to learning. A lesson for us all: Don't focus on where you fell short, look for opportunities to learn. Learn to be flexible with your strategy, and to shift tactics when a path forward is blocked. How often will the right mental attitude show us a new route to help us reach our victory condition? If we are climbing Mt. Olympus, will we need to find a new route forward to get to the peak? Never discount the power of mental flexibility, and the choice to see alternatives.

Simon Sinek, author of *Start With Why*, wrote that "Failure is not tied to money; it is a mindset. Failure is when we accept the lot we are given." Develop in yourself the attitude that you will find a way forward; you will see alternatives, and you will see the advantage in the situation that you find yourself. Failure comes not from stumbling, but from having mental rigidity. The leader and successful person need to be adaptable.

## MAKE YOUR STUMBLE A STRATEGIC PAUSE

If you are moving forward to create your success, you have surely felt the sting of the stumble. Instead of focusing on your misery, shift your perceptions. Who is around you, and where are they going? Perhaps this is your opportunity to demonstrate your talents as a leader. Develop your big heart, and help other people move forward, even as you are repairing your own situation.

The moment and period of the stumble is often an excellent time to strengthen your position in moving forward. Observe and reflect: What can you learn from this situation? Assess the route that you are taking forward: Do you need to make a shift in the direction you have chosen? How can you recharge your energy and make yourself stronger for the journey forward? Taking a moment for a strategic pause is not failing—it makes you more successful!

When I started my doctoral education—facing a five-year commitment to focused learning and writing—I was told "this is a marathon, not a sprint." That applies to so many aspects of our lives! As a leader, you can't exhaust yourself in the first six months of a transformative journey and then quit, resigned with the notion, "I tried. No one can do this." Persistence is valuable, and you must find the strategy that allows you to keep slogging forward while improving yourself as you go on. Make yourself stronger, and realize when the time is right to use your brain, your true grit, and your muscle and strength.

Your stumble can be a strategic pause that allows you to soar on your journey to success. Get ready to soar!

# What leaders do after they Stumble?

## DR. STEVE'S TIP

Expect to stumble.

Don't you wish that you could avoid it? Sometimes the way of the world—the great Tao—seems to be teaching me a lesson. I might have a plan, and I act on that plan, only to be surprised by the unexpected obstacles. I won't reach my goal in a straight line; at some point, I will probably be blocked as I move closer to what I am working on. Working toward success just seems to involve career and business lessons. I'll continue receiving the lessons until I am good enough to move on.

What should be changed may not always be obvious as you move forward. Nevertheless, if you want to be successful, you will need to learn from and adapt to your challenges.

Pay attention to what is going on. Ask yourself, "What am I supposed to be learning right now?"

When you stumble, you may be getting a signal; there is something that you should learn *and change* here. Working through a stumble may not be exciting or positive. After all, you are going through a change—and creating something new.

Ask yourself, "Is my spirit big enough to learn what I need to learn here? Will I keep moving forward?"

Let your spirit press on. Do it with a smile, if you possibly can.

# Chapter 8: Success, Career, and Right Livelihood

*While career usually has a lot to do with our notions of success, the sad fact is that many people are not happy with their jobs. Envying other's results, they may feel an urge to grow beyond their current bounds, or to change careers altogether. Maybe your first Mt. Olympus wasn't all you thought it was going to be; or perhaps you have a bigger goal in mind. How much better it would be to review your career arc, and extend it forward with a meaningful victory condition.*

*Self-image often is linked to career: "I am a doctor/lawyer/CEO, so I must be successful." The trouble is that a career can be an uncertain foundation for self-esteem—accompanied by the nagging feeling that the next level or two up is necessary to clinch the experience of success. As one advances in a career, so do the conditions for success step forward. Success can feel elusive.*

*Is it possible to feel satisfied even if your career is not yet in its optimal place? I believe it is. The person who feels successful for what exists* right now *may accelerate the arrival of other success outcomes in life. The successful person in the present likely has created a nervous system that affirms personal self-confidence and encourages the person to take meaningful career risks.*

Like many of my peers, I bought into the boomer generation mindset: "Work hard in your job, and good things will come your way. You will be successful!"

In the past 10 years, however, I have come to question this mantra. I still seek success through the work that I do, but that's no longer sufficient for me. I have shifted my thinking: Career no longer means the right job.

I will not feel satisfied unless I feel happiness in what I do. Happiness and right livelihood are a critical component of my success mindset.

As discussed previously, I believe there are four qualities to success:

1. **Success includes happiness.**
2. **Success is about financial achievement.**
3. **Success is sustained.**
4. **Success is shared.**

Without happiness, I don't count myself as a success, and I believe this concept counts for others as well. If I am going to be successful, I must work—I am creating a career that allows me to have an impact on others, helping them, and inspiring leaders. I like to work, but I don't like to be bossed around. Work gives me a chance to influence others in an organized, systematic manner, in which there are economic benefits for me.

More than ever, I am thrilled to define my career for the rest of my life.

*Right livelihood* is a Buddhist concept that can serve leaders and successful people well in the 21st century. If you are going to dedicate your passion and energy to a way of working, let your heart be fully in it. When I think about right livelihood, I check to see if my values are pointing in the same direction as the outcomes of my work. I find that I can get highly enthusiastic about my work when I think about the consequences of my actions. I want to work hard and make a difference in people's lives. I also think about the implications for my life—as I approach 60 years of age, I want to create work that reduces my stress and increases my sense of fulfillment. These choices have a significant impact on my health and well-being!

If I have actually chosen a right livelihood, then I am free to work as hard as I like. I don't have to think about other people's schedules and limitations imposed by work rules. When I have chosen a career with right livelihood in mind, then I also feel free to make my work a central focus of my life. I am happiest when my work fits my concept of a right livelihood.

So...what is *your* right livelihood?

Since you have read this far in this book, I want to share something that I am slightly embarrassed about. For much of my life, I yearned to have a corporate job. My colleague Dan asked, "Why are you embarrassed about this?" I answered, "Because I don't think I would have been euphoric with this kind of job, yet I wanted to have this lifestyle." Many of us want something we never had.

When I was growing up, IBM and General Motors were the giants of American enterprise. I admired their financial strength, their reach, and their influence on the world. I wanted to be part of something epic, and my vision of that included a corporate, multi-national experience.

With my young adult years long behind me, my vision of a successful career has shifted—a lot. Looking back and imagining myself in a corporate position? I think that would have made me miserable.

My experience has been working in the small business field. I have known weeks when I have struggled to put money in the bank account to make payroll. I remember calling managers of our child-care centers, verifying deposits for the week so that we could release checks due for essentials such as food purchases and utility bills. I remember scrutinizing repair bills and service contracts, wondering how I could reduce regular expenses in advance of extraordinary expenses—and there always seemed to be new extraordinary expenses.

**Struggle, uncertainty, and limitation.** You would hardly expect me to argue that these are qualities found in the successful career. Yet, I will tell you that there were many times in the small business world that I felt grateful to be doing what I was doing. I may not have created my perfect success; nonetheless, I had countless pleasant moments creating an uplifting culture and helping other leaders build their skills with real challenges.

A great career may involve those negative forces, because they allow a leader to emerge and make a mark, creating a meaningful success out of often-dire straits. Look for the opportunity to apply the skills of leadership and build a team founded on positivity.

In retrospect, small business leadership work was the perfect environment to teach me about developing other leaders. I had the opportunity to define my way forward—something you may have experienced during your own career challenges.

Becoming a great leader requires expanding your mind and capabilities regularly. The business practices that get you promoted to a position of responsibility are not sufficient to become a business planner or executive-level leader. Even successful people need to grow, because the conditions for sustained success require different ideas than those that got you started.

Your values may shift, as well, as you enter new phases of your life and career. For example, while I am not a fan of excessive order, the ability to expand my creative talents in writing and inspiring others demanded an organization behind me—otherwise, I could not find the time or financial backing to pursue my thoughts, explore new ideas, and reach others with them. I don't require much, but I find the discipline of a regular program of writing helps me maintain my progress. It is easier to be creative when I start with a definite structure.

The priorities that were important to us at age 20 may shift in consideration or order of preference with those at 30 and beyond. You start to think about long vacations, retirement, leaving a legacy, and health concerns—among many other factors. If you've worked for an employer for decades, you might begin to daydream about going into business on your own, without a boss or formal organizational structure. Some people go through huge shifts in the way that they work, and their vision of success changes as well.

For many of us, shifting into a new career is the cornerstone of a new success. It takes a lot of work to redefine your personal image and build a new network of people to support such a career transition. When you are determined to make a career change, entering a new field as a leader will hasten the transition. Leaders influence others and help others to join a coalition dedicated to positive change. A career change that includes leadership allows you to transfer experience and wisdom accumulated from a first career into the future.

Leaders don't have to be expert in the details, which is why leaders can emerge from the ranks of new learners. To be a leader in a new field requires a dedication to helping people, and to working for a better future. It is entirely possible to make a transition with only limited experience and yet to *lead others* because of the clarity of your vision and the determination of your purpose.

Will your career alone be enough of a success in your life? My guess is probably not—and you may have already reached that conclusion on your own. Simply doing well in a new career feels good, but it is not a sustained experience of success, and it will not make a difference to other people beyond immediate family. Career is a vital part of your life, yet the meaningful life goes well beyond service in an excellent job.

Want to look at your real career and life victories? Examine your values and the relationships that you have with the people around you.

**Review your values**. In order to create a success that's meaningful for you, decide on what is important. Put your career in support of your success. You may feel highly successful if you advance your values while you work, but if not, you may hate working. Do good work. Understand what is important to you.

**Lift the lives of those around you**. If you are working hard, you will want to know that people around you are touched by your work. Your success condition should include work that makes life better for the people near you, those people that you love, as well as people in an extended radius that you come to lead.

Your career can count for something important. Choose to be a leader in what you do—or alternatively, support another leader who believes in you as much as you believe in the leader. It is possible to contribute to a better, nicer world even as we work to pay our bills and have a life worth living. I suggest that you consider the concept of right livelihood even as you commit your effort to creating success. If a cause is important enough to dedicate yourself to it, then I predict you are on the path to becoming a leader. Whether or not you want to make that choice now, you are moving in the direction. Your leadership is needed!

## DR. STEVE'S TIP

Want to work on your career? Spend more attention to your internal compass than to pay scales, hiring reports, and industry updates. If you want to feel successful in your career, you want to be well placed. You won't feel successful in a job that's entirely wrong for you. Start with the dream you hold for your career, and examine your emotional reactions. Are you willing to pay the price to build your personal version of success?

If you have a family, that's a major responsibility—and you will not feel successful unless you share your success with them. The delicate matter of growth depends on applying your talents while minimizing risk for those who depend on you.

Let your passion and emotion come forward, and review your course forward intelligently. As a success-seeker, your mind excels at making the right decision—as long as outside forces are not forcing a decision.

# Chapter 9: Success, Lifestyle, and Personal Growth

*Have you moved closer to the summit of Mt. Olympus? Take a few moments to anticipate and enjoy the sensation of success. You have climbed to the summit, so you are exhausted, dirty, and breathing deeply. The view however — you can talk about the view for the rest of your life. You can see clouds, and nearby mountain peaks, and the landscape looking south toward Athens, east toward the Aegean Sea.*

*You have created a memory to take with you the rest of the life. Imagine the old Gods wishing you welcome, and sitting on Kronos' throne. You are now entitled to taste success. You have earned the experience.*

*Success may change your lifestyle. But unless you also transform your inner life, you'll move forward living with old anxieties and confusion. All the yachts and ballroom dances found in a season at Newport Beach won't eliminate the dragons of fear that we bring with us.*

*If you aren't conscious of your progress, you may move right past the good life without noticing it.*

*Internal change is part of the process of growth experienced by every transformational leader. Seeking success through leadership action guarantees major change from ascending Mt. Olympus; the anxieties of years' past will no longer be relevant—or visible from the peak.*

Imagine what it would be like to be Wayne Dyer. After selling a bookshelf list of bestsellers, and regularly appearing on PBS to promote personal growth and healthy living, he lives in a tropical paradise. He appears to have everything he wants—and seems to be a genuinely nice guy who's dedicated to creating a world of peace and possibility. I admire how he has worked very hard to create a lifestyle that includes idyllic experiences and the benefits of a healthy mental attitude. Even though Dyer does not own a big company or have many employees, he is a special kind of leader: a thought leader whose influence touches many people through story and ideas, rather than the command power of a CEO or a politician.

Leadership is a force that helps to create lasting success. Broaden the concept of success to include others, and consider that success comes in a variety of forms. Success is a possible outcome of working as a leader. Leadership may not be the most important factor to success, but enables it. Success is stronger, touches more people, and charges people with emotion when leadership is part of the equation for creating success.

Interested in using this leadership power for yourself? Let's examine the connection between improving your lifestyle and spurring on personal growth. Leadership and success can be part of the journey toward more vibrant living.

## LIFESTYLE AND SUCCESS

When you talk about lifestyle, are you thinking about material possessions, a home at the beach, and plenty of international travel? Certainly a gain in purchasing power can mean many new things and adventures. But the truth is, most of us can improve our lifestyle and feel even more satisfied without spending a lot of money.

A man might join a church and be part of a vibrant spiritual community. By joining this church, he expands his circle of friends. Impressed with his new connections, this man volunteers a lot of time to expand the organization's good works, and within five years, is elected to the church's board of trustees. He has now become an elder in the church and is respected by many.

A woman decides to study a martial art. She eventually earns her black belt and receives an offer to teach overseas. Afterward, she decides to write and speak about her experiences. As a result, her self-confidence soars, and she goes on to teach woman's self-defense classes around the world.

A friend of yours starts playing a musical instrument, eventually joining a community college orchestra and performing at parties and weddings. Even though it's not about the money, your friend enjoys the appreciation from being a performing musician and becomes very popular. Getting some extra spending money also affirms to your friend, "What I do is valuable!"

Do you want to improve your lifestyle? Start by thinking about what success means to you. As we've discussed, a success is some combination of these three outcomes:

1. Reaching a goal
2. Helping other people
3. Becoming more effective at what you do

Define the lifestyle you want. Keep in mind the values you are living by, and work to achieve the lifestyle that brings satisfaction to your life. Don't wait for someone to give it to you. Create your success—which includes how you will live your life.

Building your success now? Don't wait to buy your lifestyle later on, after you are rich. Find a way to enjoy all or part of your lifestyle *right now*. You may find that you feel successful immediately! Dyer teaches that "There is no way to happiness—happiness is the way." So, I'm in good company when I encourage you to choose the happiness of your lifestyle choices immediately, and work to include sustained results in your world.

Your success, happiness, and lifestyle may be as personally fulfilling as you can make it. One success may just lead to another. Why not put this principle to work in your life? Go directly for what will satisfy you, instead of waiting till the day you can afford it.

## PERSONAL GROWTH AND SUCCESS

When I was a kid, I read superhero comic books. Like legendary comedian Jerry Seinfeld, I imagined being Superman and flying; I imagined being Batman and using my wits and talents to make the world a better place. Although I wasn't gifted with superpowers, I've added new talents to my skills all the time. For me, personal growth has been all about becoming a more productive person.

I grew up with the human potential movement. It was probably a lot closer and more meaningful to me, because my dad was a practicing psychologist. Human potential was part of my family psyche. We had encounter sessions at my home, and all the trendy, superficial, and comical aspects of popular psychology were part of daily conversations. I decided early on that I would go into the family business, while a hoped-for future as a sage and lifter of lives remained in the distance—a Mt. Olympus I'd need to tackle later.

Meanwhile, I had to get my act in order.

For a while, I was a seminar junkie. I was regularly enrolled in meetings that would surely change my life. I soon came to recognize that I was doing too much navel gazing and not enough productive work. Human potential was all well and good, but I reached a point of saturation where I said to myself, "Now go out and prove yourself. You don't need to talk about this stuff for a while." So I worked in the business world.

Success has included personal growth for me. I have always wanted to add new skills, to be a rapid learner, and to be a flexible thinker. I believe that emotional intelligence is a greater predictor of success than traditional measures of intelligence. I coach others to build robust relationships with people of substance, and not to pursue *transactional relationships*. Transactional relationships, all too common in 21st-century life, exist with the assumption that I'll do something for you, if you do something for me. I encourage others to create relationships of depth rather than quantity.

How do you want to grow? Can you imagine being successful, without being changed? I suggest to you that the travel to deepest fulfillment includes the examination of your own values and priorities, and making the large and small changes that push you forward to greater happiness.

Consider that perhaps your biggest success will come from being worthy of love and respect. Instead of just acquiring material possessions, is it possible that your confidence in yourself can grow? As good as you feel about yourself now, can you become capable of more?

In the movie *The Matrix*, the lead character Neo discovers that whatever he needed to learn could be downloaded and assimilated into his persona in a matter of microseconds. Need to fight Brazilian style? Want to pilot a modern helicopter? The skills are all available on the shelf; any player can learn new skills instantaneously.

The real world offers no such shortcut. You need to choose what you need to learn and you have to work for it, while your character grows and deepens in the process.

Want to be a success? Learn to be successful. Become the dean of instruction in your own School of Life. The good news is, there's no tuition beyond sweat equity, and no time limit for graduation.

Winston Churchill wrote, "Success is walking from failure to failure with no loss of enthusiasm." Harness that mentality, starting today. You will need to change on the inside in order to earn your stripes as a leader. Your enthusiasm, your confidence, and your integrity—these are the aspects of your character that you can offer the world as emblems of your fortune. When it is real, your resonance will attract the best followers!

## DR. STEVE'S TIP

Start enjoying part of your successful lifestyle now. Just when will it be OK? If you dream of taking summer cruises on yachts near a tropical island, perhaps you can spend a week or two doing what you dream of. If you are planning to climb Olympus in the future, perhaps you can join a hiking club, learn something of Greek mythology, and practice scaling challenge mountains closer to home. You can begin preparing for your success no matter where you are.

I'm not a medical doctor, but I believe strongly enough in this principle that I gave a prescription to a physician I know, when he was lamenting that he'd never been to Hawaii. "Put the trip on your calendar for six months from now," I told him. "Make it happen."

Are you waiting for conditions to be perfect? They never will be. You can start to choose what is imperative to you, even if the portion size of your dream is smaller than you eventually want it to be.

Work on creating your success, work on leading the change, and enjoy at least some of the rewards that you are planning to add to your life.

# Appendix I: Respondent Profiles

❦

**Elaine R\*\*\***:   Owner of an advertising agency
When my son and I went into business together, we really had three goals, those goals were to find a business that we do together, that we could both get passionate about, have fun doing, a business that we could be active in the community, and a business where we could help other businesses. We were pretty open-minded. We just wanted to be in business together.

**Dan C\*\*\*:** Business Coach
I help business people choose their goals faster than they could ever do by themselves. I do that through a structured process that's designed in part by my 40 years of experience on the streets, startups in business and through the best practices of some the top business development experts in the world today. We get results in three different areas. We will always try to improve a client's productivity, which is directly related to improving profitability, if that's important, which is directly related to the quality of their life. It's not right for everyone, but for the right people it can be a very successful experience.

**Paul B\*\*\*:** Serial Entrepreneur, Business coach
I tell people that I'm kind of retired. I retired from the normal business world in 2002. I was 55 years old, and I had decided that I wanted to unleash myself from the 9 to 5 or 8 to 5 work world. So I sold my portion of a business and I retired for about two years. I hung out with my kids.

**Duane H\*\*\*:** Financial Advisor
I work for a company called Modern Woodman of America. It is a fraternal financial organization. It's a little different than most of the financial organizations you probably have heard of, like Edward Jones and stuff. Fraternal financial means it's not for profit, last year we gave $26 million back to the community. That's

the reason I joined this company, was my ability to give back to the community, be an influence in the community, and help people plan their finances.

**Susan R\*\*\*:** Professional speaker, consultant
I'm the exhibit expert. I teach people how to turn the tradeshow booth into a powerful profit center. I'm a speaker, author, event producer and an award-winning business owner who ran a tradeshow display company for 16 years, and now I speak about my expertise.

**Bill D\*\*\*:** Business owner (software)
I own a software company that provides software to the staff industry, temporary help industries. The company was started by me, 31+ years ago. We provided general software at first, and then we specialized in the staffing industry for well over 20 of the 30 years.

Owning my own business for 31 years, at least that part of my life has been successful. I've had leadership skills as an employer and prior to that a manager in other manufacturing companies. I've had to practice leadership skills; I've never had training in that area. A lot of that is just common sense and sensitivity.

**Jessica P\*\*\*:** Executive Director and founder of a non-profit, and business owner
I have a couple of different lines of business. *Career Connectors* is my nonprofit organization. So I am executive director of Career Connectors. And then I run a consulting business that has a staffing component to it and a training and development component to it as well. It's been a lot of fun and hard work.

**Rev Karen R\*\*\*:** Author, speaker, teacher
I'm a spiritual teacher with a deep passion for helping people have a joyous, peaceful, collaborative, stress-free, and orderly relationship with money.

**Dr. John K\*\*\*:** Physician
I am a radiation oncologist, which is a physician that uses the discipline of radiation therapy to treat patients; most of them are cancer patients. I can also use radiation therapy for nonmalignant disease conditions. I came out of residency training and took the position with the private practice group that I'm still with today.

**Dave C\*\*\***: Sales professional, speaker

I basically have two passions. My historical passion has always been about helping businesses with their sales challenges, going in and providing leadership as well as a sales force, strategies and plans for executing their growth initiatives.

Lately I've been doing a lot of work with my passion, which is helping people discover their adversities (real or perceived), and helping them work out the places they desire to go. That whole background stems from my experiences of my youngest son's heroin addiction and how his adversity pulled me into a rabbit hole and how I worked myself out of that by riding a bicycle.

**Karen M\*\*\***: Nonprofit leader, consultant

I am Karen the caring connector. I wear a lot of hats; I am a TV spokesperson and advocate for peace. I am part of a movement to break the cycle of violence and abuse, so I frequently speak on TV and radio to educate and to provide information for people who are, or might know of someone who is a victim of domestic violence or abuse. I am also a spokesperson for causes, so I am aligned with a lot of nonprofits and charities. I really excel at fundraising and activities; and leveraging people coming together and serve.

**Clark P\*\*\***: CEO

I'm CEO of TeleSphere, which provides cloud communications. Our charter is transforming the way businesses communicate. In the past, all communications meant buying a piece of hardware. We're taking all that intelligence and putting it into the cloud. As long as the client has access to our network, they don't need that hardware anymore. Whether it be a PBX that used to run your phone system—with our customers there is no PBX. They have an IP phone on their desk; it goes out through a connection to our services and then all their phones to the things that they do because of our intelligence in the cloud without having to duplicate that office after office with a box.

**Simer M\*\*\***: CEO

I am the CEO of Valor IT; we have another company we have acquired, Ace Global. I am president of that as well. We have about 650 people total and growing—successful I guess!

**Teresa D\*\*\***: Speaker, author, business council chair, influence expert

I am an international speaker sought by entrepreneurs and large corporations wanting to better understand how local gossip can suddenly turn into epidemic word of mouth.

As the Chair of the Evolutionary Business Council, I lead an international, invitation-only council of speakers and influencers dedicated to teaching the principles of success.

**Patti S\*\*\*:** Marketing and business consultant
I am what they'd call in the old days, a business consultant. But today I'm a business trainer. I trained in conventional business marketing methods and how to boost your business on the Internet. So my basic title is business and Internet trainer.

**Deborah B\*\*\*:** Banker
I run a line of business for National Bank of Arizona. That is the wealth strategies line of business, a line of business that caters to the high-net-worth individual. Not only from the banking products: loans and deposits, but also from an investment standpoint. I'm an executive with the bank and also on the bank's board.

**Stephen H\*\*\*:** Author, speaker, consultant, philanthropist.
I'm a philanthropist. And what I do is I champion trees and children. I believe that there is a connection between them, and it hasn't been explored enough and exploited enough in how they are complementary to each other. Trees are for life. Children are for life, and they both bring life to each other. And so, my work is built around funding a minstrel ways fund, the Calgary foundation. The money that I raise outside of what I need to take care of myself is channeled into that fund to support the growth of that support of trees and children programs that will exist and will exist in the future. I do that through organization culture related work, culture works, and teams; how do you bring productivity improvement to groups and teams using managing and leading is the focus, that I'm working from at this point.

**Dr. Larry E\*\*\*:** Dentist, Speaker, Author
I was trained as a dentist, I worked as a dentist for 30 some years, and was successful at that. A good part of that time I was moving myself into becoming a professional speaker. That's what I really enjoy doing, that's what I'm good at. So for a good part of that dental career, I was also speaking.

So when an opportunity came along to sell my dental practice and move more into professional speaking field, I did that. So for the last five years, I have not been a practicing dentist. I have been practicing part-time on and off. I've been dedicating myself to the speaking career, and writing and consulting world. These are things I enjoy doing.

**Sharon L\*\*\***: Author, CPA, consultant
I look for ways to help people improve their lives, primarily in the financial and success arena. I want to make sure that what I do adds value to their life and is affordable.

I want to make a difference, not necessarily on the backs of other people, but as a result of other people's success.

**Chris H\*\*\***: Venture Capitalist
Right now I'm involved in a number of different boards locally, and in advisory roles. I retired from a company that I ran for seven years, three months ago.

**Amy G\*\*\***: Executive Director of a large community nonprofit
My title is president and executive director of the Boys and Girls Clubs of Metropolitan Phoenix. I work with the Board of Directors and the staff to fulfill our mission, which are kids and clubs. When the schools are closed, we are open. It is after school care. We have about 20,000 kids in our clubs operating in five cities. We also operate a dental clinic just for kids. We raise the money for that. Essentially what I do is make sure that we have enough money—we take care of the kids.

**Ed S\*\*\***: Author, speaker, association executive
I taught at Arizona State University for quite some time, the business college, at the Center For Executive Development, the management training department. That's where I got involved in a lot of association management. There was a professional group called ASTD and I also got involved with the National Speakers Association, and also another affiliation with Meeting Professionals International, which has about 23,000 members around the world. ASTD has about 60,000 members around the world, this chapter used to be the second-largest chapter in the country.

After I left ASU several years ago, I got more involved in training and speaking and got more involved in the association business. I come mostly from the academic background. I taught marketing, retailing, communications and management development programs as well.

We have a few books, my daughter was involved; we put a few books out together and she wrote five or six by herself.

**Jack T\*\*\***: Attorney, serial entrepreneur, author
What I do now is promote the book that I just wrote, which is titled *Employ Yourself Now, Enjoy Yourself Now: Seven steps to start and operate a business in less than 90 days.*

**Chris J\*\*\***: CEO of a marketing agency
I tell people that I'm the chief cat wrangler. We are a professional services business. We are people who are delivering services to other people. It can go really well some days and be chaotic other days.

**Terry B\*\*\***: Restaurant Owner (four locations)
What I do is wear a lot of different hats in the restaurant; day to day operations of our four restaurants. So I'm working at each one on a daily basis. When I go to work, I am at all of my restaurants; I don't just go to one. I've been to two of the four today, and I will probably be at all of them at least once or twice the rest of the day.

So I'm there to make sure that any staffing issues, operations issues, executions, service, coaching, teaching, training, I get to do a lot of those things.

**Stacey F\*\*\***: Internet Entrepreneur
My brother and I started an internet security company about three years ago. We have just sold that company to another company here in San Francisco. Now I am working on something in advertising technology.

**Ryan R\*\*\***: Financial planner
I run a wealth management firm. I have been a financial planner myself for the last 13 years, and also responsible for recruiting, training and motivating a team of associates here at the office.

**Patrick M\*\*\***: Product manager
I'm a product manager at Disney Social. So we specialize in free-to-play games that are on Facebook, IOS, Android, Windows, any-

place there is platform gaming going on. It's software. I live in Palo Alto, part of the Silicon Valley, it's very interesting because most of the software you hear about is the most talked about. It's actually very beneficial for my development, being here.

**Michelle M\*\*\*:** Speaker, author, entrepreneur, physician
I am a retired family physician; I have a company called "Am I Hungry?" which has a mindful eating program; we use the ancient concepts of mindful eating to help with the modern problems of an abundant food environment.

As part of that I have the opportunity to speak professionally, I have written several books, and I have a training company. So I train other people to teach the workshops that I developed.

**Felix N\*\*\*:** Security consultant, entrepreneur
I work in workplace violence prevention. I coach leaders and other decision-makers how to prevent workplace violence. I provide high-level advice; assist in the development of policy, plans and training.

**James S\*\*\*:** Author, entrepreneur
I think of myself as an entrepreneur, a professional speaker and a citizen servant. I've done public service; I also try to serve my breakfast.

**Kirk M\*\*\*:** IT consultant
I run my own consulting business doing IT consulting and doing programming and database and all of that, mostly for pharmaceutical companies. I started the business back in 1993 so we are officially 20 years old this year.

**Suga R\*\*\*:** Poet, educator, writer
I live my life to the fullest, I live full of joy, and happiness. I am always striving for more, striving to be better, striving to be greater, striving to express myself fully, all of my talent to achieve all of my goals and live all of my dreams.

I will say I'm a peace activist, I'm an educator, I'm a mentor, I work with parents and families who lost their loved ones to tragedies, murder, suicide, I'm a poet, I'm a writer. I'm currently a student at Farm School NYC, a two-year certificate program in urban agriculture.

**Ronnie P\*\*\***: Editor in Chief

I'm the editor in chief for the Association of Clinical Research Professionals. That means I am in charge of the journal called *The Monitor*, which is a publication by clinical researchers for clinical researchers. So I make a difference by healing clinical researchers to reach one another with their own progress in their own jobs, things that they have learned that make their jobs easier, better, more streamlined, more efficient, more accurate, more ethical and they help one another that way.

Since clinical research is so critical for everyone, for health care that means a lot to me personally and it means a lot to the rest of the world, because clinical research is what brings us cures for diseases and treatments for diseases we haven't got cures yet.

**Bob B\*\*\***: Speaker, author, trainer, lawyer and Past President of Toastmasters International

*Bob's longer answer is missing.*

# Appendix II: Recommended readings for leaders and successful people.

*Not all respondents recommended a book.*

ELAINE R***

**The Bible**
**Walk the Walk: The #1 Rule for Real Leaders, Alan Deutschman, 2009**

I am an active reader. I read a lot of books.

If I had to think of a book that has impacted me the most on success strategies, I would choose **the Bible** because there are so many examples. No matter where you are in life, failing or succeeding, there are stories available that would give you an example of how to be successful in that different situation.

On the micro, that's like a big, big book on success. Recently I read the book **Walk the Walk.** Walk the Walk is making sure that your values and your idea of success are in line with what you are doing about every day.

It's very powerful, it has some powerful case studies about real-time companies, and how they have identified the core things that are most important to them. On that they have driven their success based on core values.

DAN C***

**Think and Grow Rich, Napoleon Hill, 2010**
*Think and Grow Rich.* Napoleon Hill. I've read it every year for 30 years.

PAUL B***

**See You At The Top: 25th Anniversary Edition, Zig Ziglar, 2009**
I am really a voracious reader. I probably read about 20 books a year, minimum. That's usually a four-to-one ratio for non-fiction

versus fiction. I really love books, particularly historic-based books. The book that stands out, which I've probably read five or six times, is *See You at the Top* by Zig Ziglar.

I read that book in the early '80s. At that time, I had accomplished a lot of my financial goals. I felt very, very good financially. This book inspired me to expand my horizon well beyond just financial goals.

I quoted Zig Ziglar yesterday, they needed someone to offer words of wisdom at the end of a Toastmasters meeting. I volunteered. One of the ones I love is "When you do more than what you are paid for, soon you are paid more for what you do," which is right out of that book. I have to say that book continues to influence me.

## DUANE H***

### Good to Great: Why Some Companies Make the Leap...And Others Don't, Jim Collins, 2001

I've read a lot of books actually. I live my life on a lot of quotes.

A couple of them I got from basic training when I was in the military. One of them is "slow is smooth, smooth is fast." That one is one I try to live my day by. More or less it means take your time and do it right. If you take your time you don't have to do it over again.

When I was in construction that was something people didn't understand: "No, let's hurry and get done." Well, when you mess it up and have to do it over again, so much for hurrying!

Another one a drill sergeant called it the 5 Ps, it's actually the 6Ps: Proper planning prevents piss poor performance. That's one of my favorite quotes.

I had to read *Good to Great* when I was in Iraq, and I also read it in my capstone in college. It's a really great book, which talks about helping a company go from being a good company to a great company.

It's something you can apply in your personal life just by taking a look at the concepts. One of the concepts I took was "Wash your cottage cheese." They interviewed a guy, training for a decathlon, or a triathlon, or something, burning 12,000 calories a day. "What do you do to be better than anyone else?" "Honestly it's doing the little things. I wash the fat off the cottage cheese before I eat it." That's really what being a good leader is—it's just doing the little things. Being successful is doing the little things every day.

## SUSAN R***

**The Five Temptations of a CEO, Anniversary Edition: A Leadership Fable, Patrick Lencioni, 2008**
*The Five Temptations of a CEO*, that's about management and leadership more so than success. I did find that book fascinating; it was a gift. It sort of sticks with me.

## BILL D***

**Autobiography of a Yogi (Self-Realization Fellowship), Paramahansa Yogananda, 1998.**
I think the first step in any endeavor is to form a consistent basis on how you define it. I didn't plan on it, but when I was handed *Autobiography of a Yogi*—reading that book helped me to establish that standard. Certain rules about the goals I go after and, what is my intention? And making so that those are consistent intentions applied in whatever part of my life I happen to be focusing on.

## JESSICA P***

**The Five Dysfunctions of a Team: A Leadership Fable, Patrick Lencioni, 2002**
My favorite author is Patrick Lencioni. *The Five Dysfunctions of a Team* is the first one I've read of his, with a fictional team and a new CEO that comes in and takes over. It's a really great book. Then he wrote recently *The Advantage* which is more of the process behind how you get to the successful team. He takes the ideas he discussed in *Five Dysfunctions of a Team*, and lays it out in the process. It's not as interesting, but he lays out the steps that it's necessary to get there. I've seen him speak over and over—I really relate to him because of the style in the way he talks to his clients in the way he moves them along.

## REVEREND KAREN R***

**This Thing Called You, Ernest Holmes, 2002**
*This Thing Called You*, by Ernest Holmes. It's a spiritual book; I consider it a love letter from the universe to us. It's one of my favorites.

## DAVE C***

**Save the World & Still Be Home for Dinner, Will Marre, 2009**

Lots of books have influenced me. My most recent favorite is *Save the World & Still Be Home for Dinner* by Will Marre. The author talks about all the issues and problems that exist in the world. There really isn't one answer that's going to solve all the world's problems. What's going to solve the world's problems is people's ability to recognize who they are, being comfortable in who they are, not being an actor, and in that authenticity and honesty, allow them to act to change the world around them. For me, that goes back to my definition of success. Because when you're doing those things you are touching, you are connecting, you are communicating, you are helping others and that's reinforcing that notion that my difference in the world is being me and I'm truly being a successful person, because I've used everything I've been given.

## KAREN MALTA

**The Alchemy of True SUCCESS: * Activate Your Mind *Revitalize Your Body *Reignite Your Spirit, Jaden Sterling, 2013.**
**The Four Agreements: A Practical Guide to Personal Freedom (A Toltec Wisdom Book), Don Miguel Ruiz, 1999.**
**How Did You Do It, Truett?: A Recipe for Success, S. Truett Cathy, 2007**

I think leaders are avid readers. The first important book that comes to mind was from a dear friend of mine, a successful author, Jaden Sterling. He is a wealth master and a true caring connector. The name of his book is *The Alchemy of True Success*. It's relatively new but very, very, very powerful on many levels. It describes and lovingly walks people through all components and aspects of having wealth, abundance, success in their life.

The other one is that famous one called *The Four Agreements*.

I also love John Maxwell and his books. One of my personal heart-centered heroes is Mr. Truett Cathy. He is the leader of the Winshape Foundation and also the CEO and founder of Chick-fil-A. I love his book *How Did You Do It, Truett?*

He has a great sense of humor. I think leaders should have a great sense of humor.

## CLARK P***

**Good to Great: Why Some Companies Make the Leap...And Others Don't, Jim Collins, 2001**

**Execution: The Discipline of Getting Things Done, Larry Bossidy, Ram Charan, Charles Burck, 2011**

Once I really thought through that I decided on "My Mom's Book of Life." She's done a lot of things. She taught me early on that mediocrity was never something to aspire to, or settle for. I think really watching her life, and knowing her expectations, and seeing her example of what's she's achieved. It's worth paying that price to do those other things.

The way she lived her life is probably the biggest contributing factor to my own success—as far as an external resource.

## SIMER M***

**Moments Of Truth, Jan Carlzon, 1989**

**The Dream Manager, Matthew Kelly, 2007**

**Mastering the Rockefeller Habits: What You Must Do to Increase the Value of Your Fast-Growth Firm, Verne Harnish, 2011**

I believe for an entrepreneur, the books are critical. I didn't believe that four years ago, but reading books has changed my life and I think our business is really built around these books. One is *Moments Of Truth*; it is focused on every touch point you have in your business and how every moment of truth that you have in kind with an employee and community is a promoter, and enabler. It is an opportunity to show them what you really can do and cannot do. It changed our life here.

The other book is *The Dream Manager*. We are starting the dream manager here, we are interviewing for a dream manager role, if you know anyone that really wants to help people achieve their potential help them achieve their dreams, it's part of our value too, really admiring our people and helping our people to achieve their potential.

*Mastering the Rockefeller Habits*, our entire KPI's and our entire dashboards are built around measuring the Rockefeller Habits. It's an everyday tool for us.

## TERESA D***

**The Power of Focus: What the World's Greatest Achievers Know about The Secret to Financial Freedom & Success, Jack Canfield, Mark Victor Hansen, Les Hewitt, 2000**

**A Return to Love: Reflections on the Principles of "A Course in Miracles, Marianne Williamson, 1996**

I'm an avid reader. So I would have to say there is a long list of books that have supported me. Probably one of the first that I ever read that really got to me was the *Power Of Focus* by Les Hewitt. It really helped me see if I could get really intentional with my actions, it would make a profound difference. And probably not far on the heels of that, I started reading Marianne Williamson, who wrote *A Return To Love*. It really got me focused in on the notion of really following my own dreams. Following my own passion is not only in my highest interest, but it is also in the highest interest of the world for me to do what I was put here to do. I think when I look at the practical learnings of some of the more spiritual and philosophical learnings, Marianne Williamson's work, I think that really made some profound shifts in my life.

## PATTI S***

**The Slight Edge: Secret to a Successful Life, Jeff Olson, 2005**

The book that I carry with me, almost like *the Bible,* is Jeff Olson's *The Slight Edge: Secret to a Successful Life.* My trainings go almost verbatim out of what he believes in, and when I found it I thought, wow, here's a person who is almost on the same thinking mindset businesswise as I am. I always go back to that book because it just confirms what I teach and what I believe. What better book would that be? You know what I mean? You're right there.

I'm always learning. Each week, I look at it again, and it's a different kind of a slant. It's an amazing book—a bestseller kind of book you have to have on your shelf kind of deal.

## STEPHEN H***

**The Aquarian Conspiracy: Personal and Social Transformation in Our Time, Marilyn Ferguson, 1987**

### The Turning Point: Science, Society, and the Rising Culture, Fritjof Capra, 1984

I go back to the very first book that fell off the shelf into my hands—literally. I was in Kampala, Uganda, to build an HIV education program for the country of Uganda. And the book, *the Aquarian Conspiracy* by Marilyn Ferguson written in the '70s, fell into my hands because I needed to find a new way to look into the world, which could be this notion of success, could be the purpose or to achieve notoriety. This book fell toward me, and I read it, and it turned me 180 degrees toward the work that I was doing, to look at the world in a very different way. It's the book that started it.

And if you ask what book came next, or anything like that, it would be this myriad of books because that's what prompted me to come back and do my doctorate. I did my doctorate that combined quantum physics and metaphysics, all-in-one area. So I read widely, from that point on.

Then it was the Fritjof Capra book, *The Turning Point*, and a lot of other related books that just started speaking about this other way, the biocentric view the world versus the anthropocentric view of the world; so I considered doing forestry, outdoor recreation, environmental recreation, geography—these all started reading true, the things that I've been learning, but I hadn't started putting them together terms of success in business and success in managing and leading. That is when I started to shift gears.

## LARRY E***

### How to Win Friends & Influence People, Dale Carnegie, 1998

I read constantly. I had a hard time nailing this down. Most books that I remember the best of the ones that were recently. I'm 61 years old. The older books have influenced me now.

Looking back, I couldn't come up with one book. Certainly, reading a lot and being open to new ideas; one of the talents I have you seeing all the new possibilities. I've been able to consult and lecture people on where the future might be going and how to use these new things. And so there's a lot of influence with that.

One book that did influence me a lot was Dale Carnegie's *How to Win Friends and Influence People.* Enormously influential book for me, I've read it several times, that helped me and empowered me in many ways. He did exactly what *Mt. Olympus* is all about: He interviewed a lot of people, he found themes, and within those themes he told stories. Telling his stories was huge, because you got to know his people and what they were doing.

Most of the books I've read on business and management, and were meaningful, did that. They had stories. They were not just facts. It put a human face on it. More than saying, "the three steps of management are..." Instead, "John had a problem... Here's what he did. Here's what he learned from that."

## SHARON L***

### Think and Grow Rich, Napoleon Hill, 2005

Absolutely, Napoleon Hill's *Think and Grow Rich*; written in 1937, over a 100 million of them have been sold around the world. And the reason it stands apart from any other book is it is like the thesis paper—the term paper—for success because it wasn't just one man's philosophy. Hill interviewed over 500 successful people, the richest men of the time and talked to thousands of people who consider themselves failures. What he created in his 25-year journey was the basis of the book, *Think And Grow Rich*. So it really is the commonalities that he found in all successful people and the stumbling blocks of the people who considered themselves failures.

He pulled that together. And so anyone can understand the elements of success to improve their life.

I love it when someone has a copy and it's all dog-eared with notes in the margins and all highlighted.

## CHRIS H***

I've read a number of books. I wouldn't say there is one book that stands out. But there is a poem—"If" by Rudyard Kipling—that I encourage everyone to read because I think that's the most profound leadership statement in a work of art that's been compiled.

In a lot of ways, I think that covers a lot of leadership elements. So I have it on my wall and my kids have it on their wall as well. I refer to it quite often.

## AMY G***

### Life and Death in Shanghai, Nien Cheng, 2010

Colin Powell is my favorite author. I've read a couple of his books, but there is one book that is not a leadership book that is my favorite book of all times. It is a biography, it is a story. It taught me a lot about leadership and what type of person is a leader. It is called *Life And Death In Shanghai.*

It's my favorite book—I've probably read it five or six times.

It wasn't a typical 10-step program for leadership. It was a biography, a true story, and can you imagine being in prison by yourself as an elderly woman or an older woman, not knowing where your daughter is, not knowing about your home—everything was taken!

Everything—just gone! One day she's sitting there having tea, the next day she's in jail! A room a third of this size, no toilet paper, no bed, no nothing. And she had stuff in China. It taught me about her being a leader within her world. All those skills she had to survive.

## ED S***

### How to Win Friends & Influence People, Dale Carnegie, 1998
### The Greatest Salesman in the World, Og Mandino, 1993
### The Success Principles(TM): How to Get from Where You Are to Where You Want to Be, Jack Canfield, 2006
### Primal Leadership, Daniel Goleman, Richard Boyatzis, Ann McKee

Written way back when, Dale Carnegie's *How to Win Friends and Influence People* still has some great lessons that are relevant for today's society.

I've been a fan of Og Mandino's work for long time. *The Greatest Salesman in the World* is one of the top sellers, in sales it is just next to the Bible, it's been around forever.

Jack Canfield has several books out that are worth reading. I do a lot of reading in the self-help section, I'm interested in emotional intelligence, and Daniel Goleman's book called *Primal Leadership*. There are some good lessons in that too.

I'm always learning, picking up new things and new ideas.

## TERRY B***

**In-N-Out Burger: A Behind-the-Counter Look at the Fast-Food Chain That Breaks All the Rules, Stacy Perman, 2010**

**Pour Your Heart Into It: How Starbucks Built a Company One Cup at a Time, Howard Schultz & Dori Yang, 1999**

I've read a lot of restaurant books—in particular about In and Out Burger and Starbucks. I really enjoy reading books that talk about similar situations to ours. And Schneider's I believe from In and Out, they started out as husband and wife with a little spot and they grew as something that continues to be an amazing product. To be able to get to that level doesn't happen overnight, it takes a lot of time; I'll talk to my wife and talk about the length of time that it took to get to that level. We've been open five years; they've been around for 60-plus years. That's the book that I read, and I read over and over.

## STACEY F***

**Never Eat Alone: And Other Secrets to Success, One Relationship at a Time, Keith Ferrazzi and Tahl Raz, 2005**

One of the biggest things in my life and in my experiences that has helped me be successful, and helping my brother be successful too, is the relationships and the network we have.

*Never Eat Alone* by Keith Ferrazzi is all about networking and how to build your network of people. It has helped in terms of meeting the right people and having the right mindset of meeting those people who have helped me be successful.

## RYAN R***

**The 21 Irrefutable Laws of Leadership: Follow Them and People Will Follow You, John Maxwell and Steven Covey, 2007**

I was turned onto a book by a man named John Maxwell; over the past six months I have run into him in different facets. I have a study group; we have managers across the country in different offices that get together once a month over the phone for a conference call, sharing best practices and ideas. Maxwell was brought up—and *Laws of Leadership* is probably one of the better books; it touched on a lot of good points. It taught me some new things and refreshed on older ideas.

## MICHELLE M***

### The E-Myth Revisited: Why Most Small Businesses Don't Work and What to Do About It, Michael Gerber, 2004

It might seem funny, but to me the book that had the greatest influence was a little book called **E-Myths**—the entrepreneurial myths—a book that I read early on in this process. It was important for me because I was a physician for 16 years before I retired to run my company full time.

There was about a 7-year overlap between my medical practice and running my company. I think at first I had this great idea for these workshops and I was going to try to do this. That book really helped me see that what I needed to do was build a business. The way to build a business is to create processes and create manuals for everything that I could to get written down, and to start building a team.

That book really helped me create a larger vision for what was possible.

## FELIX N***

### FM 22-100 Military Leadership, Department of the Army, October 1983
### Principle-Centered Leadership, Stephen Covey, 1992
### The Audacity of Hope: Thoughts on Reclaiming the American Dream, Barack Obama, 2008

I am an avid reader of virtually everything I can get my hands on that has to do with leadership and success. Going back to my formative years as a young reserve, non-commissioned Army officer, the one book that opened my eyes to the realities of the importance of being prepared to lead people was an old Army publication called *Military Leadership.* It talks about three things that were very basic and fundamental to a young sergeant and what they needed to know: how to be, how to know, and how to do. If you could master those three simple words, you can then look at the mirror and say I can do my job without feeling inhibited, intimidated, or threatened; I am confident with myself, and if I am confident with myself, I don't have to invoke authority to influence people. I get influence by portraying myself as having confidence and the ability to shake the outcome.

I love Stephen Covey's *Principle-Centered Leadership* and the books that he has written on highly effective people. I love John Maxwell and his book on how to personally involve yourself in becoming an effective leader.

I recently read Barack Obama's view of *Audacity of Hope,* his story of his dream and vision, and how this led to being the president of the United States.

## JAMES S***

**The Bible**
Like I thought a lot about this one. No, I read all the time but there is not one book. I could state a few books that everyone will state are highly influential. Like Shakespeare, everything is in there somewhere. *The Bible*: everything is in there somewhere. For me it's just reading. Primarily biography is individuals and art and politics and business and picking up things from those.

## RONNIE P***

**The 7 Habits of Highly Effective People: Powerful Lessons in Personal Change, Stephen R. Covey, 2013**
You might say that it starts with the sublime and goes from there. I find the most in *the Bible* and the life of a saint I try to imitate, because he has been successful. Also I have found in my career a lot of help in Stephen Covey's *Seven Habits of Highly Effective People*.

## BOB B***

**The E-Myth Revisited: Why Most Small Businesses Don't Work and What to Do About It, Michael Gerber, 2004**
When I first started my own business, I read a book by Michael Gerber called the **E-Myth**, which stands for entrepreneurial myth. The first chapter asked, "What do you want on your tombstone?" If you could sum up everything on your tombstone, what would it be? What is your legacy? It goes back to the long-term perspective of success. How can I do that? That's what would be on the tombstone. I think it's interesting that I've gotten into estate planning. I talk about how dead people don't own stuff. Everybody has the same fate—it's just a matter of when. We're all just

pushing the ball down the road. And if I can push the ball down in a better way, I have made a difference in the big picture. The context of Gerber's book: What do you want on your tombstone? Your business should help you accomplish that. It's not just making money.

# Appendix III: More Leadership Behaviors that Support Success

Working on your success? My success informants told me what leaders do to become successful. Here are the most frequent answers, by category.

- Believing in your decisions, having confidence
- Creating a team
- Living by values
- Helping other people
- Being consistent/persistent
- Working from a vision

These six behaviors were described in Chapter Six. These were not the only answers that I heard, but they were the answers that I heard most frequently. If you want to make an impact on your success list, these are the ones to concentrate on!

What is a leadership behavior? Leaders do many things that the rest of us do. These leadership behaviors were mentioned by my respondents as noteworthy. The work of leaders influences others and creates changes in the world. Leadership behaviors have the potential to create positive shifts around us.

Here are some of the other leadership behaviors that I heard in my interviews. These were mentioned less frequently as the behaviors in the first six:

**Pay Attention to Communication Skills.** A person with communication skills expresses ideas verbally and through technology, and is a good listener. People like to talk to a person with good communication skills. This kind of leader makes you feel valued.

From Chris, CEO of a marketing agency:

> I have a lot of conversations with employees that are one on one, where they are nervous, and they are trying to figure out the right way to tell me something they don't want to

tell me. There are challenges you have in getting past that, to get to what we are really talking about.

**Lead by Example.** Many people have told me that leaders need to show others how to act. Many people feel inspired when they see their leader doing exactly as they asked the followers to do. Some people call this "walking the talk." Leaders, people watch you every day to be sure you mean what you say!

Stacey, who created an internet social media company, told me:

> If you want people to stay in the office long hours to finish pushing out a feature, you need to be there with them, sitting with them, getting this feature out. You can't say, "Oh, I have a meeting," or "I have to leave." You have to lead by example.

**Be Disciplined**. The disciplined leader does the hard work first. He or she understands priorities, and assigns time to get large and small things done. The work is not always convenient or "fun," but the tasks and effort are handled. Some people talk to me about "leading yourself." Being a disciplined leader could be described as "leading yourself."

Ryan, a successful financial planner, emphasized discipline.

> I think to be a leader you have to have a lot of self-discipline. I think that's the one leadership skill that has helped me to be successful, makes me be accountable to more people than just myself.

**Inspire Others**. The words and actions of a leader have the power to lift the spirits of others. The leader's character by itself often adds inspiration to the lives of other people. Many leaders become practiced at public speaking because of the inspirational quality of their work.

Ryan told me that leaders must be inspirational, "Be sure that you are going out there and inspiring other people to be successful."

**Practice Time Management**. Leaders and successful people are conscious of the value of their time. Effective people arrange their work so that they get results. The successful people in my world choose to understand and work in favor of their priorities.

Stacey had a lot to say about time management:

> In terms of running a team or building a product, there are lots of things that can easily get in the way. Pick the things that are going to have the most impact, either to you, or a customer, or a relationship that you know you are going to need. Manage your time so that you are doing things that are absolutely vital.

**Be There First.** By definition, leaders often are the first to achieve something meaningful. Leaders are known for getting out in front, and establishing the forward momentum. Leaders can motivate others to push forward with them because of their commitment to stake out a forward position.

Patrick, a product manager for a Fortune 50 company, explained this principle:

> Someone just needs to go in and figure it out. Be that first person; take charge and lead. That has really helped me. If you can be someone that leads people into the unknown, if you are the first person into the unknown before everyone else, then you are an expert in the unknown.

**Have a focus.** Successful people can focus on their work. Focus is a quality of mental activity that sets a priority for attention. Leaders and successful people do get distracted. Being distracted is part of being human. Part of success is returning to the object of focus when it is important.

Patrick told me how a leader's focus can direct the work of the team:

> You can have the best team in the world as far as executing things, but if they don't know what they are supposed to execute, they can't do anything. If people don't know what the goal is, they can't be successful.

**Be mindful.** A mindful person observes the thinking process. When choices are made, the successful person is aware of bias or preference. Decisions are conscious. Impulsive action happens to all of us, but the mindful leader is informed about the impulse, and may pause before a bad decision is made.

Michelle, an entrepreneur and physician, reminded me that this is often hard to achieve:

> Mindfulness is having awareness - being aware of what you are doing, and why. We hope to be aware at all times or at least with the goal of being aware. It is not possible to be aware at all times.

**Be flexible.** Find another way to reach the goal! Successful people adapt, they know what is important. A flexible person is willing to revise a course of action if it helps them achieve more without losing sight of their goals.

Felix, a business owner, told me:

> Even when you are working with a superior who you don't get along with, find ways of creating a win-win situation. Even though it may be difficult; create an amicable solution.

# Appendix IV: Collecting Data About Leadership and Success

*Success means different things to different people. So does leadership. Expand your horizons – talk to a broad range of people about your success journey.*

Napoleon Hill, renowned author of *Think and Grow Rich*, worked to interview successful people at the direction of one of the most successful people of his time. Based on an introduction by Andrew Carnegie, Hill spoke to 500 people and generated his theory of personal achievement and success. Carnegie challenged Hill to use his own resources and his own wits to meet these successful people with Carnegie's introduction. Out of these interviews, Hill articulated 13 principles that form the basis of his theory of the pursuit of success.

*Leading the Way Up Mt. Olympus* was not designed on the basis of Hill's research method, although I have read his book several times. Instead, I have been inspired by the research techniques coming out of qualitative social science, using an approach called phenomenology, to collect and understand life experiences. The German philosopher Martin Heidegger developed the organizing ideas that have evolved into modern phenomenology, which I studied with my advanced research on leadership. Heidegger's work Being and Time (1927) launched the discussion of phenomenology.

This book and the inquiry into success have many similarities to Hill's work, especially the close attention paid to the real experiences of people who have been there. I have found it inspiring to talk to so many people who have found their own version of success, and have led people in the process. I love hearing these kinds of stories! This book has been a work of passionate love... when I hear about other people's challenges and their successes,

I remember that great things are possible for me. My hope is that you will feel the same way!

## METHODOLOGY: HOW WERE THE SUCCESS INFORMANTS SELECTED?

The top requirement for being included in this study were that the respondents (the people I interviewed) had to describe themselves as successful. In addition, these people agreed with the statement "I used leadership skills to create my success."

The process started with phone calls, connecting with people within my social network, either part of my LinkedIn network or through personal introductions. The scientific term for this process of collecting respondents is a "convenience sample."

I did not meet all of the respondents. I had phone chats with people who lived in another city. A few of the respondents lived in Canada.

Another objective in selecting respondents was to create diversity. I wanted to talk to wealthy people, but I also wanted to talk to people who are doing good things in the world. I wanted more, for example, than a sterling group of successful real estate agents who represented a similar world view. I made an intentional effort to talk to many different people in my sample.

I intended to explore what success is, without prejudging it. I needed to talk to people who had seen success from different vantage places. I believe I succeeded in collecting different kinds of voices, with vastly different experiences.

Selecting a sample of 35 different people also guaranteed that I would have some differences in the success thinking. This sample was not huge, but it was big enough to be respectable for social science research. With a large enough sample, the data collection effort is sure to contain a broad collection of viewpoints. I have taken every effort to document my findings objectively in order to inform people interested in success and leadership.

## MEANING OF WORDS

The concepts of leadership and success are complex. Reasonable people differ on what these two words mean to the reader and speaker. I recently read a scholarly article that suggests that many people commonly confuse the concepts of "leadership," "management," and "command." Clearly, the concepts of leadership and success can evoke different meanings for people who do different kinds of work. Our experiences color our expectations about these words.

So, when I asked people if they were "a leader" or "successful," how did I define these words?

I never did. Not by oversight, however: When asked "What do you mean by success?" and "What kind of leaders are you looking for?" I always answered, "I am talking to people who consider themselves a success. I am talking to people who consider themselves a leader." I wanted to hear from those different voices, not just to collect the ideas of people who thought exactly like me. Nor did I want to talk only to CEOs and millionaires in my sample – although I have included those people in my sample.

Exploring the meaning of words is informative. I listened to my respondents in order to expand my understanding of the important words based on what others told me. I am willing to add meaning to what I know, and I suspect my readers want to do this as well.

## THE INTERVIEW PROCESS

I recorded interviews with my respondents. I told them to speak all they wanted, but not add more than they had to say. If they did not know what to say, we could move on quickly. These are the questions I asked:

1. How do you define success?
2. What book taught you the most about success?
3. Who helps you to be successful?
4. How do you help the people who help you?
5. How do you influence other people?
6. How do you find opportunities?
7. When have you stumbled? Have leadership skills helped you move past this point?
8. Are you still learning? If so, what are your learning goals?
9. How have leadership skills helped you be successful?
10. Are there any leadership skills that have been most important for you?
11. What leadership skills do you emphasize for your followers?

I provided the questions two or three days before the date of the interview, in order that the respondents could have the questions with a fresh perspective.

Several of the respondents clearly had prepared answers before our interview. I observed several of the respondents referring to their answer sheets as we proceeded through the interview. Others seemed to be entirely spontaneous in their answers. I did not notice a difference in the answers from those who had prepared for the interview—other than it seemed to make more efficient use of our time.

I asked follow-up questions when I wanted to explore a topic in greater depth. I tried to keep the interview almost entirely about what the respondent had to offer, rather than my opinions. Sometimes, however, I was so interested that I needed to ask follow-up questions.

Interviews were held in respondents' offices, and at public places. When clients lived out of state, I arranged conference recording through the web-based service Free Conference.

Most interviews took between 20 to 45 minutes. A few interviews were considerably longer.

## HOW WERE THE QUESTIONS FORMED?

I had an idea about where I wanted this book to go; I started with a single question, "How do people use leadership skills to help them become successful?" From this question, I produced a short list of questions that would help me explore this concept.

I then tested these questions on three respondents. Their answers did not end up as part of the research set reported in this book. However, I gave additional thought to the questions that I started with, and made a few revisions based on the experience of asking real people.

I focused my attention on building questions that were clear. I wanted to have questions that did not confuse my respondents, or my readers. Clear questions could help to illuminate my subject, and I hoped, would help to suggest non-cliché answers from my respondents. I wanted fresh answers, so I looked for questions that were non-routine.

I also wanted focused, supportive questions that directed all thinking to my essential issue: What is the linkage between leadership and success? I believe my questions challenged my respondents to dig a little deeper in their answers. I did not press hard on my respondents when they did not have a specific or tight answer. I did pursue an exact ordering of questions to force my respondents to drill further into their own truths. I wanted to collect thoughtful answers.

More than one respondent told me, "These are really great questions!" I was pleased to hear that because I wanted to be successful in reaching the core ideas for my informant group. When they said, "Great questions!" I took that to mean that the respondents were challenged by them—I was making them think, getting beyond the trivial and into the meaningful.

## HOW WAS THE DATA TREATED?

The treatment of data is an important question, because, in the data-analysis phase, I sought out meaning from the collective answers of 35 people. I paid attention to the standard responses; I also looked for individual approaches. I realized very quickly that I had a lot of data available for my transcribed interviews, and narrowed my focus to three secondary questions:

1. What does success mean to leaders?
2. What leadership behaviors helped a person become successful?
3. What do successful people do after they stumble? What leadership skills were employed to help a person keep moving?

The first of the three focused questions deals with the meaning of success; the second of these examines leadership behaviors; and the third deals with perseverance through challenges. The first two questions are throughout the transcript materials, as multiple questions discussed the concepts of "success" and "leadership." Only one of the interview questions specifically examined "stumbling."

As I looked for themes expressed in the interviews, I created conceptual "buckets" to store sections of text illustrative of each topic. Some buckets had a lot of material; others had only a few examples. I was interested in the buckets that contained many examples, as these indicated large areas of respondent discussion. When there was agreement from a large number of respondents, my assumption is that this is important information. My plan was to select the five largest buckets of themes for each secondary question, and to explore what this means for leadership and success. I then would do my part to interpret the meaning in the published form of this book.

**Everyone agreed**. All of the respondents agreed on two major issues in this exploration. First, all the respondents told me "I stumbled." I heard this message repeatedly: The path to success does not come easily; expect to stumble.

Second, all respondents agreed that they are still learning. Amazing! I was impressed that 35 people from different professions and lifestyles could agree on not just one, but two points. Nevertheless, successful people (who are leaders) told me "learning is important – I do it every day." Why was it, though, that only a few could name specific learning goals? Perhaps most of us are uncomfortable or unfamiliar with talking about what we are learning.

**Look at the data buckets.** I clipped portions of text from interviews that followed a theme. Reviewing each transcript, I paid attention to the "meta" message of each respondent. I often found multiple themes expressed in a single block of transcript—after all, we can embed a lot of meaning in a few short paragraphs.

Not surprisingly, I found that some respondents discussed certain themes repeatedly. I believe this process demonstrates how the human mind works: When we have been impressed with wisdom, we tend to talk about it regularly. Buckets quickly overflowed with data when a few respondents discussed a theme substantially.

I was more impressed with a theme when a high number of interviewees discussed it. Hence, a single respondent might talk about one issue for 20 minutes, generating a large bucket of information. When a respondent introduced the idea in an interview, I considered it like a "vote." With more votes, an issue is valued highly. If 10 respondents discussed an issue, it implied a great deal of value—compared with a single respondent who spent more time discussing the issue than 10 others put together.

**What does it all mean?** Clearly, success and leadership can mean different things. Without ruling out important ideas, I have paid attention to what people say when they discuss these words. I have been excited to discover that when leaders discuss success, for example, they mean one of three ideas: meeting goals, helping people, and becoming more effective and powerful in the world. (See Chapter 4 for more discussion about this topic.)

My choice has been to focus on the ideas of the respondents, and to create a synthesis that can help all of us look at different ideas and find a meaningful way of working and living. You can find this work of synthesis in the later chapters of the book. I am interested in helping other people create their successes and work as leaders. Ultimately, I believe that leadership skillfully employed is an act of service that helps other people. The synthesis of ideas in this book is intended to be a service to help readers live and work more effectively. We start this process in this book by examining the ideas of the respondents.

## WHAT IS PHENOMENOLOGY?

Phenomenology is a means of gaining knowledge from human experience. We can gain knowledge from the scientific method, learn knowledge from reading the works of philosophers, and perhaps we can gain knowledge through religious experience. The phenomenologist recognizes that human experience is valuable, and often not systematically studied. The failure to study human experience is regrettable, as we collect wisdom and learning from other people (parents, job trainers, mentors, teachers) without trying to sample from the larger world.

I applied the method of phenomenology when preparing my doctoral dissertation. At the time, the word sounded exotic. As I looked at phenomenology further, I found value in searching for the meaning level of human experience. I have chosen to be a friendly voice, and an informed one, for sharing this information with others.

As discussed above, philosopher Heidegger was focused on understanding what the nature of being is. He encourages us to look at experience and human cognition as a means of understanding being. In this work, I have connected the experiences of successful people and discuss what success is, what leadership is, and how an individual may build a life of meaning while pursuing a goal-oriented life.

I believe this is important. The experiences of others can inform us. We need not adopt another person's set of priorities and values; nevertheless, through the applied study of success and leadership, we can encourage others to lead lives that impact many other people positively. It remains for each of us to use the energy and focus to sustain a life of transformation and fulfillment.

## HOMAGE TO NAPOLEON HILL

For decades, people have studied Hill's work. Hill used a form of applied phenomenology, although his work does not use that term. Hill seems to have anticipated the philosophical approach to building knowledge! He worked for many years to describe and interpret his understanding of wealth-building, and to create his 13 success principles. Countless people have applied these principles in their lives, in the hopes of "growing rich."

I am pleased that I could work in the manner of Hill, and I acknowledge the similarity in our approaches. I did not intentionally begin this work as a similar study to Hill's work. While there is an essential similarity, let's examine a few differences.

Hill studied the financially wealthy, such as business tycoons and other people who had created wealth in their lifetime.

I applied no financial test to my study group. I believe that success can have a broader meaning, and that people can work very hard to achieve success that is not exclusively about financial independence. How does one study success without a clear definition? I believed that was part of my objective: to ask others what success mean to them.

I reject the idea that success means reaching the age of 65 with $2 million dollars in the bank or any other definite attainment. One can have a fulfilling, successful life without a significant access to funds. Conversely, the media tells us frequently about wealthy people who are dissatisfied with their lives and relationships. I am interested in seeking a life worth living—this is a successful life to me.

Unlike Hill, I selected my respondent group. I shared the selection process with others I trusted. Toward the last half of my respondent-selection process, I asked others for help in locating successful people. Others volunteered names to me when my research purpose became known. I shared the choice of successful people with others; the process used in choosing respondents has been guided by other's opinions.

I do not know if Hill used an interview protocol. I decided that a set of standard questions would allow me to target my research to a few salient points. I did ask some subjects follow-up questions, especially when I was curious about their career experience. I believe this process of digging deeper into the life experience helps to illuminate the point. At the same time, the structure of each interview was built around the same set of questions, so the answers represent a focused inquiry. In all likelihood, Hill used some questions repeatedly with his respondents, and expanded these with interested conversation. (Wouldn't it be wonderful to have observed Hill in his interview process?)

In several ways, my purpose in creating this book was less ambitious than Hill's. He wanted to develop a practical science that could help others become rich, and I make no such claims about this work. I believe it is valuable to learn from others, and to discover what people mean as they describe becoming successful. The ideas discussed in this book can increase the chances of becoming successful. Everyone may need to have the right mindset, the right attitude toward living and serving others, and success may follow.

Hill did not write about leadership. We do not know if he felt that leadership could be a contributing factor to becoming successful. I suspect that if I could talk to Hill, his concept of leadership would seem outdated to me; the concept of leadership has surely evolved in the nearly 100 years since he wrote about becoming rich.

Words change their meaning over time. Even as our words change, the meaning and attitude toward big ideas evolve as the decades flow past us. This study works to understand the linkage between leadership and success in the early 21st century. I have no doubt that in 50 years, these words will have shifted some of their meanings. The perspective on the world changes as our history and technology gives us new ways to look at words and values.

Individuals seek to grow in their affluence, to be well regarded, and to accumulate power. I have grown up with an eye for completing new achievements, and I suspect that most of my readers have felt the same thing. It is natural for people to want to feel successful, and to expand their influence over their community. This is what leaders and persons do in order to advance their lives. People seek success.

Over time, success may mean different things. In Hill's era, success may have just meant "riches." Perhaps in the next century, a successful life will only mean having abundant spare time and a rich social network. As Heidegger has taught, the meaning of human life is associated with the times in which he or she lives.

## DR. STEVE'S TIP

Phenomenology is the study of human experience. By listening to what other people think of life issues, we can learn a great deal about what it means to be human. Perhaps we can expand the possibility of leading an enriched, happier life through other peoples' examples.

I have chosen to study leadership and its relationship to success. I have applied a systematic method for collecting first-person experiences, and through this book, I have brought you a synthesis of the discussion.

Imagine what remaining questions about human experience and consciousness are still unsettled:

*What does it mean to fall in love?*

*What does peace mean to people?*

*Why do people change their minds about race?*

*Why do people follow violent religious leaders?*

*And countless others, of course!*

Human experience is worth studying. Phenomenology concerns itself with discovering the meaning and motivation to life. I choose to explore the meaning of leadership through the experience of different people's lives. The same tools can be applied to many other important questions.

# About the Author

❦

Steve Broe is a leadership coach and university professor who writes about people changing their lives at work.

He was born in Southern California and moved to Arizona in the early 1990s. He has two adult children and is joyously married to Carolyn, stolen from the seaside city of Newport Beach. He operated a family business for 30 years, and started a charter school organization in the mid-1990s.

Steve has practiced the martial art of Aikido, which taught him to appreciate balance and vitality in the way he works, moves, and thinks. He has also been active in Toastmasters International, which values excellence in speaking, thinking, and leading. He also is an amateur musician, playing the bass clarinet.

Steve's first book, published by ProQuest in 2009, was an academic dissertation that examined how U.S. military veterans view the leadership challenges in schools. In 2012, he published *Leaders in Transition,* which asks—and answers—the question, "How do people change careers and become leaders in the process?"

Steve teaches organizational behavior and leadership for the University of Phoenix and Grand Canyon University. He lives in Scottsdale, Arizona.

You can contact Steve Broe through LinkedIn, Twitter (@DrSteveBroe) and through these websites:

www.SteveBroe.com

www.Mycareerimpact.com

I would love to hear from you and send you my monthly newsletter, *The Renaissance Leader!* Request a free subscription by email from sbroedtm@gmail.com.

Made in the USA
Charleston, SC
25 May 2015